ROOTS, DEEP AND STRONG

Great Men and Women of the Church

by
Mary E. Penrose, O.S.B.

illustrated by Mary Charles McGough, O.S.B.

PAULIST PRESS
New York/Mahwah, N.J.

Cover Design by Jim Brisson.
Cover illustration by Sister Mary Charles McGough, OSB.

Library of Congress Cataloging-in-Publication Data

Penrose, Mary, 1924-
    Roots, deep and strong : great men and women of the church / Mary Penrose
        p.   cm.
    ISBN 0-8091-3538-8
    1. Christian biography. I. Title.
BR1700.2.P46 1994   94-39377
270.1′092′2—dc20   CIP
[B]

Published by Paulist Press
997 Macarthur Boulevard
Mahwah, NJ 07430

Printed and bound in the
United States of America

Contents

iii

Acknowledgements

Strictly speaking, the writings of the Fathers/Mothers in the Faith belong to the public domain. However, I wish to thank Reverend Johannes Quasten, editor, and Walter J. Burghardt, SJ, co-editor of the **Ancient Christian Writers** series, and William B. Eerdmans, Jr., publisher of the **Ante Nicene** and **Post Nicene Fathers** series, for their permission to use and edit quotations from these works. I am also grateful to Sister Agnes Cunningham, S.S.C.M., who indirectly initiated this project many years ago, and to Father Lawrence Boadt, CSP, who carried it to conclusion with the assistance of his genial Paulist Press staff. My thanks, also, to my long-time friend and co-worker, Sister Mary Charles McGough, OSB, whose sketches greatly enhance the book. Finally, I am deeply grateful to my friends Lou, Maureen, Louise and Ramona whose tangible and constant support of me and my work over the years has been an indispensable ingredient in the final product.

DEDICATION

In memory of my friend Carroll Stuhlmueller, CP, who now enjoys the company of the Mothers and Fathers and whose persistent prodding and gentle encouragement helped make this book a reality.

Foreword

There are certain moments in life that one never forgets. They are times of a seminal experience that seizes the inmost core of our essential self and leaves us forever transformed.

A good number of years ago, I stood for the first time on the rim of the Grand Canyon of the Colorado River. I will never forget that experience. The adventure began before dawn as I shivered in the chill, early spring air, waiting and watching for the first touch of light to awaken the colors of that unbelievable wonder. I spent the day following the sun around the rim of the canyon, until the darkest night poured silence into that great, open space, pushing the warm air of its depths up to embrace the shining stars as they came tumbling down from the sky. The moment had been unique. My horizons were never again to be the same.

Several years later, in a classroom in Lyons, France, I had another seminal experience—one I have been able to describe only in terms of the Grand Canyon. In a "moment" that began in October 1963, I encountered the Fathers and Mothers of the Church. Once again, the horizons of my world were shattered and I have never been the same since. Just as I traveled around the rim of the Grand Canyon, looking, reaching out, absorbing, contemplating, wondering, praising, so I have sought to examine, explore and probe the hearts and minds of Clement, Ignatius, Macrina, Paula, Justin, Irenaeus, Radegund, Hildegard and the others who make up that great company. The day of my adventure with them has not yet come to an end. I have not ceased to marvel at the depths of their faith and love and wisdom, their

1

holy indignation, their gentle, compassionate and, at times, humorous humanism.

The Benedictine Sisters, during the years of our association in Mundelein, Illinois, joined me on occasion in my patristic exploits. As we shared and exchanged treasures—they, of their life and art and prayer; I, of the fruit of my study, reflection, teaching and research—we were mutually enriched. That enrichment remains, despite our absence from one another.

This publication is a sign of a new adventure with the Fathers of the Church and our Mothers in the Faith. It belongs rightly to one of the daughters of a saint who admonished all his children to "read our Fathers in the Faith" (Rule of St. Benedict, ch. 72). The contents of this book have been chosen judiciously and advisedly, with keen intuition, affection and respect for the men and women whom we cherish as friends and teachers in the "traditioning" of the faith that comes to us from Jesus and the Apostles.

It is hoped that the publication of this book will facilitate and foster access to the writings of these women and men for those who would not ordinarily have such access. I am delighted and privileged to be given this opportunity to congratulate Paulist Press for its publication, a project which may lead many others to the "rim of the canyon."

Sister Agnes Cunningham, S.S.C.M.

Introduction

All of us have desires within which seep through to our consciousness with more or less intensity and frequency over the years. One of these, the search for roots, has been evidenced in recent years. Among ecclesiastical scholars it brought about a surge of special and enthusiastic interest in knowing more about the history of our early ancestors in the Church. My own curiosity about this phenomenon was the first impulse I had which led me, eventually, to compile the biographies found in this volume. The more I read from the sources, the more the "voices" of our Mothers and Fathers in the Faith compelled me to study their personalities and thought further. But I could not keep these discoveries to myself.

I decided to make the richness of our ancestors available to those who had neither time to read, nor money to buy their complete works. It was my hope, also, that those who wished to do a more thorough study would find this small study a spur for further pursuing this fascinating subject on their own. My goals, obviously, required making some decisions. I wanted to reach readers who, though not scholars in the strict sense, were looking for something more than could be found in current popularized and sometimes pietistic works available on the market. In other words, I wanted it to be an in-depth work while, at the same time, not ponderous or over-ladened with historical details irrelevant to modern readers. On the other hand, I was not willing to sacrifice basic content or historical accuracy. As a result, I have included historical incidents and/or any complicated controversies of the times only if they have significance in relation to the person portrayed.

Finally, because I wanted to emphasize the incidents and thoughts in the lives and works of these ancient writers which resonate with our own, I chose those aspects of their lives which could put readers in touch with the enthusiasm and faith of the early Church, with its problems and joys. Most of all, hoping to touch the inner heart of readers, I incorporated select, direct quotations from our ancestors in the faith. Their living words, after all, are the strongest witness we have to the heritage which they have left us. May we all be blessed with their courage and wisdom.

Sister Mary E. Penrose, O.S.B.

CLEMENT OF ROME

The Mystery Man

The "Apostolic Fathers," Christian writers of the first and early second centuries, are very important witnesses to the faith because they were either in personal contact with the Apostles or had received instructions from their disciples. They give us a picture of the Person of Christ still vividly remembered and express doctrines taught in the very early days of the Church. They did not, therefore, aim at giving a scientific exposition of the faith nor did they develop doctrine; they simply repeated doctrines given by the Apostles.

"Envy and strife have overthrown great cities and rooted up mighty nations." Are these the words of Jeremiah? Abraham Lincoln? Winston Churchill? John F. Kennedy? What is your guess? Wrong, if you named any of those just listed. That small sentence was spoken by a man who, tradition claims (from information supplied by St. Irenaeus), was the fourth pope in the history of the Church. In the familiar canon of pre-Vatican II days, he followed after Peter, Linus and Cletus; his papacy extended from around 91-100 A.D.

If Pope St. Clement of Rome were suddenly brought back to life, we might be a little nervous about his identity. Very little is known about him. Origen and Eusebius, the great historian, identified him as the fellow worker mentioned by St. Paul in his

Epistle to the Philippians whose "name is in the book of life" (4:3). Others say he was Titus Flavius Clemens, cousin of the Emperor Domitian. These claim he was put to death "for Jewish practices," along with his wife, Domitilla, who was probably a Christian.

Finally, some give another twist to this latter version of his life by saying he was a Jewish Christian. This seems unlikely. However, if he were Jewish, he must have been a Greek Jew as it is clear from his writings that he was well acquainted with the literary and cultural life of the late first century. The Basilica of St. Clement, one of the earliest parish churches in Rome, may have been built on the site of his home, but neither the place nor the manner of his death is certain.

With such flimsy and seemingly conflicting evidence, we may wonder how St. Clement won such esteem in the early Church. We do know that his origins were early enough to merit for him the title of "Apostolic Father" along with Ignatius of Antioch and St. Polycarp. Though other writings have been ascribed to him, "The First Epistle to the Corinthians" is the only one authenticated as his own. According to St. Jerome and Eusebius it was written by Clement in the capacity of a representative of Rome.

Historically, the Epistle precedes the letters of St. Ignatius, which makes it the earliest writing of the Fathers of the Church. It resembles St. Paul's letter to the Philippians and was considered such an important document that St. Clement of Alexandria included it in the New Testament Canon. This indicates that it was thought to be an inspired work and was read in many churches during that era.

The exact date of the Epistle is controversial. Though written during the time of a persecution it is not certain which one, that of Nero (c. 68 A.D.) or that of Domitian (c. 97 A.D.). The evidence swings more favorably toward the latter date. Clement speaks of "sudden and successive calamitous events" which made him tardy in writing the letter, and some of his terminology is definitely militaristic in tone.

The immediate purpose of the letter, a rebuke to those who, without ecclesiastical authority, had deposed presbyters and instigated factions within the Church at Corinth, recommends the type of obedience exemplified in "soldiers to their leaders." Though Clement exhorts with firmness, he does so with fatherly concern. There is evidence that the letter was well received and that it achieved its purpose.

WHAT DOES THE LETTER HAVE TO SAY TO US?

The Epistle is important also for us in the Church today. As an ancient document it testifies to the martyrdom of Peter and Paul in Rome and gives us a description of the primitive government of the Church of Rome as well. From it we learn that there was in existence an hierarchical order in which the laity had no part. In fact, this seems to be the first time the term *layman* is used: "The layman is bound by the laws that pertain to laymen."

Clement indicates further that the hierarchy was divinely instituted and he includes an explicit declaration of apostolic succession. Though the Epistle does not explicitly argue to the primacy of the bishop of Rome, neither does it deny this belief. In the letter, the function of the bishop is always seen in the context of worship, a facet in the life of the Church which tended to become obscured in later ages. The role of the bishop in the early Church was that of minister of the altar, not that of an administrator of a diocese. Fortunately this ritual character of the bishop's office is coming into more prominence in our day.

Contemporary with the writings of St. Ignatius of Antioch, Clement's letter, like those of Ignatius, was concerned primarily with unity in the Church. The writings of both are early and strong witnesses to the Church's monarchical form of government; both see liturgy as central to the life of Christians, attest to belief in Christ's divine nature, and affirm that Church officials do not derive their authority from the people but from God. The two men differ only in their approach: Ignatius, in his letters, speaks as a friend to friends; Clement speaks as a father to his people.

THE HEART OF THE MATTER

"The First Epistle to the Corinthians" is important not only as a valuable historical document, but it also gives us insight into the heart of this man of mysterious origins. One can see, even in his description of such a legalistic subject as the hierarchical structure of government, the real source of his pastoral concern: the peace and harmony of the Church which he regards as the body of Christ. In a lyrical passage he cites the peace and order of the universe as exemplars both of the formal and informal structures governing humans. Some scholars think that one section, a beautiful prayer for peace near the end of the letter, was an ancient Eucharistic canon which Clement had composed to be used for a Sunday liturgy.

What does the Epistle convey to modern Christians? Two things in particular: a lesson on love and unity for an ecumenical age and, as is clear from the opening sentence of this article, a lesson on moral rectitude for an age torn by the discord of moral corruption and of brother rising against brother. Clement highlights for us the Christian virtues of charity, piety, obedience, hospitality, humility, and penance. The motives he gives for practicing these virtues are the example of Jesus ("...let us fix our gaze upon the blood of Christ") and the saints, the blessing Christ gives to us, the promises of future life, the order and harmony required in the universe and the discipline needed for our own lives.

From our contemporary frame of mind, we might well take to heart the following sayings of St. Clement of Rome:

—**Let us honor the aged among us.**

—**Let us train young men in the fear of God.**

—**Let the strong not despise the weak, and let the weak show respect to the strong.**

—**Let us esteem those who rule over us.**

—Let us clothe ourselves with concord and humility.

—Our children...must learn how effective with the Lord is a humble frame of mind.

—Since all things are seen and heard (by God) let us fear him and forsake those wicked works which proceed from evil desires.

—The good servant receives the bread of his labor with confidence; the lazy and slothful cannot look his employer in the face.

—Seeing, therefore, that we are the portion of the Holy One, let us do all those things which pertain to holiness, avoiding all evil speaking, all drunkenness, all seeking after change, all abominable lusts, detestable adultery, and execrable pride.

ST. CLEMENT ON THE RESURRECTION

Let us consider, beloved, how the Lord continually proves to us that there shall be a future resurrection, of which he has rendered the Lord Jesus Christ the first-fruits by raising him from the dead. Let us contemplate, beloved, the resurrection which is at all times taking place. Day and night declare to us a resurrection. The night sinks to sleep, and the day arises; the day again departs, and the night comes on.

...Let us consider that wonderful sign of the resurrection which takes place in Eastern lands, that is, in Arabia and the countries round about. There is a certain bird which is called a PHOENIX. This is the only one of its kind, and lives five hundred years. And when the time of its dissolution draws near that it must die, it builds itself a nest of frankincense and myrrh and other spices, into which, when the time is fulfilled, it enters and dies. But as the flesh decays a certain kind of worm is produced, which, being nourished by the juices of the dead bird, brings forth feathers. Then, when it has acquired strength, it takes up that nest in which are the bones of its parent, and bearing these it passes from the land of Arabia into Egypt, to the city called Heliopolis. And, in open day, flying in the sight of all men, it places them on the altar of the sun, and having done this, hastens back to its former abode.

...Do we then deem it any great and wonderful thing for the Maker of all things to raise up again those who have piously served him in the assurance of a good faith, when even by a bird he shows us the mightiness of his power to fulfill his promise... Having then this hope, let our souls be bound to him who is faithful in his promises.

IGNATIUS OF ANTIOCH

God's Wheat

St. Ignatius, another Father of the Church meriting the title, "Apostolic," was the third bishop of Antioch. The only information we have about him, other than seven letters attributed to him, are scanty bits from the writings of St. Polycarp, St. Irenaeus, Origen, St. Jerome and the historian Eusebius. Ignatius wrote his letters en route from Antioch to Rome where he was sentenced to die during the reign of Trajan (98-117 A.D.). As soldiers transported him by land and sea to Rome, they passed through various cities where Christian communities had been founded. The holy bishop became acquainted with these Christians and later wrote to them as well as to the Christians in Rome and to his friend St. Polycarp.

Whether St. Ignatius was actually martyred or not is not known, though his letters on the way to Rome certainly indicate such a death was in store for him: "...I am prepared for fire, wild beasts, the sword, or the cross, so that only I may see Christ my Savior and God who died for me." St. Polycarp infers that he did endure martyrdom in a letter written to the Philippians. This letter constitutes the most important evidence we have arguing to the authenticity of Ignatius' own letters. The contents of these letters, precious enough, have great historical value as well, since they must have been written no later than fifteen or twenty years after the death of the last Apostle.

Because so little is known about St. Ignatius, it is understandable why occasional legends came into existence in order to
honor him. One of them claimed that he was the little Jewish
child singled out by Christ in Matthew's Gospel as a model of
childlike simplicity; others suggested that his name, *Theophorus*
("God-borne"), indicated that he was the child carried in
Christ's arms in Mark's Gospel. But legends are legends and the
real saint comes through in his letters. There is a similarity
between the letters of Ignatius and Polycarp, but Ignatius teach-
es us more about the early Christian mentality and his style is
fiery, abrupt and impetuous. Polycarp writes in a calm, sedate
manner, comparable more to the writings of Clement of Rome.

As a bishop, Ignatius saw himself as the responsible teacher
of the faithful; he believed that to be in communion with one's
bishop was to be safeguarded against error and heresy. The
chief heresy he himself had to deal with was Docetism which
declared that Christ's human nature, and therefore his passion,
death and resurrection, were only make-believe, not factual.

It is in the writings of St. Ignatius that we find the term
"Catholic Church" used for the first time to designate that body
of those declaring themselves Christians. His spirituality can be
said to be a combination of St. Paul's ideas of "union with
Christ" and St. John's notion of "life in Christ." In Ignatius it
resulted in a life-style of "imitating Christ," with martyrdom
being seen as the ultimate and most perfect form of that imitation. In fact, it can be said the *becoming a disciple* of Christ constituted the prayer of his life.

The topic of Christian unity was almost an obsession with
him. He reiterated to his people: "Be preoccupied about unity,
for nothing is better than this. Help others along as the Lord
helps you." This unity comprised the bulk of his message, though
he did deal with other matters as the following passages indicate.
They are filled with idealism as well as amazing good sense:

**And so, put on the armor of forbearance and refresh
yourselves in faith, that is, in the body of the Lord; and
in love, that is, in the blood of Jesus Christ.**

IGNA-
TIUS
of
ANTI-
OCH

Do not let your lips be for Jesus Christ and your heart for the world.

A Christian is not his own master, but waits upon God.

Find time for unceasing prayer. Ask for more wisdom than you have. Keep your spirit awake and on the watch.

Copy the ways of God in speaking to each as an individual person.

There is no thanks for liking good pupils. The real task is by mildness to bring to obedience the ones who plague you. Not every wound is healed by the same remedy.

Stand firm like an anvil under the hammer. A great boxer will take a beating and yet win through. We ought to put up with anything especially for the sake of God so that he will put up with us. Become more zealous even than you are. Understand the age in which we live.

As this last passage indicates, Ignatius, a man of sterling faith, was also in tune with the times. It seems he was also in tune with ours, for he was quoted as an authority at least thirteen times in Vatican II's document on the Church, **Lumen Gentium**. The words for which he is perhaps most famous describe how he saw himself at the end of his life. In this passage, he begs the Romans not to prevent him from the final and most perfect form of imitation of Christ, martyrdom.

I write to all the churches, and impress on them all that I shall willingly die for God unless you hinder me. I beseech of you not to show an unseasonable good will towards me. Allow me to become food for the wild beasts, through whose instrumentality it will be granted me to attain to God. I am the wheat of God, and let me be ground by the teeth of the wild beasts, that I may be

found the pure bread of Christ. Rather entice the wild beasts, that they may become my tomb, and may leave nothing of my body; so that when I have fallen asleep in death I may be no trouble to anyone. Then shall I truly be a disciple of Christ, when the world shall not see so much as my body. Entreat Christ for me, that by these instruments I may be found a sacrifice to God.

Whether Ignatius actually became food for wild beasts or not is not certain, but it is certain that his whole life was one of doing Eucharist!

POLYCARP

Bread for Baking

If St. Ignatius of Antioch saw himself as God's wheat transformed into pure bread for Christ, St. Polycarp could have considered himself baked bread. The reason? This early Christian martyr, instead of being ground into flour by the teeth of wild beasts, was thrown into a fire, though his body remained unburned. That he, like so many of his martyred contemporaries, yielded an abundant harvest for the Church is attested to not only by his name, which means "fruitful" or "rich in fruit," but also by his life. His story follows.

We have few sources of information on this remarkable saint, but those we have are invaluable as historical documents. There is his own letter, "The Epistle to the Philippians," considered the best historical evidence we have on the authenticity of the letters of St. Ignatius. It is evident that he had St. Ignatius in mind when he wrote it. He refers to him indirectly at times and even uses expressions peculiar to his friend. We also have a document, "The Martyrdom of St. Polycarp," a letter which is an eyewitness account written by the Christians of Smyrna recording the death of their holy bishop. Finally, we have a letter written by St. Ignatius to his friend.

Little is known about the ordinary facts of Polycarp's life. The date of his birth is uncertain. In "The Martyrdom" he is recorded as saying he had served Christ for eighty-six years. Since he was a Christian through baptism and no one knows whether he was baptized in infancy or later, this number of years affords scant evidence as to his age. There is similar doubt about the date of his death, though both February 22, 156 and February 23, 155 A.D. have been proposed. Nor do we know when or by whom Polycarp was assigned to the bishopric of Smyrna (located in the center of the west coast of Asia Minor), though St. Irenaeus tells us he was consecrated bishop by the Apostles themselves. Because of this some conclude he must have been rather young at the time of his appointment.

Fortunately, we learn much about Polycarp from the letters of Ignatius. He says, "Polycarp, you have been abundantly blessed by God...I was glad enough to learn that your mind is grounded on God as on an immovable rock, but I rejoice exceedingly to have been able to see your face. May its candor be a joy to me in God." The comment refers to a visit Ignatius had with him en route to Rome during the last days of Trajan's reign. Later in the same letter he says, "The age is in need of you if it is to reach God–as pilots need the winds and as a storm-tossed sailor needs port."

An indirect source of information is a letter written by St. Irenaeus about St. Polycarp to a third party. In it he records his own awestruck youthful encounter with Polycarp and the latter's first-hand acquaintance with the Apostle St. John: "...I can speak even of the place in which the blessed Polycarp sat and disputed, how he came in and went out, the character of his life, the appearance of his body, the discourses which he made to the people, how he reported his intercourse with John and with the others who had seen the Lord." It is Irenaeus, too, who records Polycarp's dealings with Docetism, which, as we have seen, denied the reality of the Incarnation and, therefore, the value of the redemptive work of Christ. Upon meeting the Docetist, Marcion, who asked if he recognized him, the saint retorted, "I recognize you as the first born of Satan!"

In his "Epistle to the Philippians," we find that Sacred Scripture was so woven into the fabric of Polycarp's life that it is difficult for the reader to discover what is uniquely his own thought. He stressed two points over and over again in this letter: the necessity of purity of faith and the need for shunning avarice, that is, the love of money which is the root of all evils. As he exhorts his readers to holy living, he uses persuasion through an appeal to the pride they have in the founder of their community, the first Christian settlement on European soil. He humbly asserts, "...neither I, nor anybody else like me, is able to keep pace with the wisdom of blessed and glorious Paul."

THE MARTYRDOM

It is in "The Martyrdom of St. Polycarp," a document giving the oldest detailed account we have of the martyrdom of a single individual, that we come in contact with the heart of this saint. Because of its antiquity, the document is often called the first "Acts of the Martyrs." It is also the earliest evidence we have of a cult of the martyrs. On Polycarp's death, the document records, "We afterward took up his bones, more precious than costly stones, and more excellent than gold, and interred them in a decent place. There the Lord will permit us, as far as possible, to assemble in rapturous joy and celebrate his martyrdom—the day of his birth!"

The account of his death reads like a novel and sounds like a majestic symphony with one mighty theme running throughout: the passion of Christ. The step by step similarity of his death and the death of Jesus is remarkable, since, for the most part, the document can be verified as being authentic. If film-makers ever discover his story, it could be a thriller on TV!

At the height of persecution, Polycarp's friends persuaded him to leave Smyrna. They hid him on a nearby farm. Three days before his arrest, he had a vision during prayer which gave him a premonition of the kind of martyrdom he would undergo. He saw a pillow under him burning with fire and so he declared, "I must be burned alive."

A slave boy, turned informer under torture, revealed Polycarp's hideaway to his persecutors. The writer of the account is careful to note that, like Jesus, Polycarp was betrayed by a member of his own household. Another similarity occurs in his capture: "...mounted policemen set out on Friday at about suppertime, armed in their usual way, as though they were in hot pursuit of a robber." Nor was a final comparison to the Lord lost by the writer: "...the moment of departure arrived, and seating him on an ass, they led him into the city. It was a great Sabbath." And was it coincidental that the chief policeman's name was Herod?

When the proconsul tried to dissuade him from his purpose, Polycarp imitated Christ's freedom in accepting death. Rather than take the oath to "swear by the genius of Caesar" and revile Christ, he said, "You threaten the fire that burns for an hour and in a little while is quenched, for you do not know the fire of the future judgment and of eternal punishment, the fire reserved for the wicked. But why do you delay? Come, do as you wish." He exemplified this same freedom in his immediate preparation for death. We read:

When the pyre was prepared, he laid aside all his clothes, unfastened the loin cloth, and prepared also to take off his shoes. He had not been in the habit of doing this, because the faithful always vied with each other to see which of them would be the first to touch his body. Even before his martyrdom, he had always been honored for holiness of life. Without delay the material prepared for the pyre was piled up round him; but when they intended to nail him as well, he said: "Leave me just as I am. He who enables me to endure the fire will also enable me to remain in the pyre unbudging, without the security afforded by your nails."

After he recited a prayer, the fire was lighted. It was then that the witnesses reported the miracle: "The fire produced the likeness of a vaulted chamber, like a ship's sail bellying to the breeze, and surrounded the martyr's body as with a wall; and he was in the center of it, not as burning flesh, but as bread that is baking, or as gold and silver refined in a furnace!" Because his body would not burn, the executioner was forced to complete the martyrdom by stabbing Polycarp with his dagger.

The document records further that Herod's father tried to persuade the magistrate not to give Polycarp's body to his

friends. His reasoning was that they would abandon their worship of the *Crucified* and replace it with devotion to the martyr
instead. Providentially, this incident has left us with a passage
indicating clearly the distinction made in the early Church
between devotion to Christ and the veneration paid to the
saints. Polycarp's friends declared, "They did not realize that we
shall never bring ourselves either to abandon Christ, who suffered for the salvation of all those that are saved in the whole
world...Him we worship as being the Son of God, the martyrs we
love as being disciples and imitators of the Lord."

In addition to the valuable historical information we gain on
the devotional life practiced in the early Church, what else can
we learn from Polycarp's life? If he has not been named the
patron of "joyful old age" he clearly deserves the title. But more
than this, his persevering courage in the face of torture and
death is encouragement for us in the little daily deaths we have
to undergo. He knew, literally, what was worth dying for and
what was not worth his precious time.

His great concern for the growth of the Church might give
him the right to be called the "patron of catechists" as well. As
soon as he had to go into hiding, he continued his custom of
praying for the Church day and night. And in him we find the
tenaciousness of many early Christian martyrs who tried to win
converts right up to the end, even among their persecutors. Like
St. Paul, Polycarp, when asked to deny Christ, replied to the proconsul, "I am a Christian! If you wish to learn the teaching of
Christianity, fix a day and let me explain!"

PRAYER OF ST. POLYCARP ON THE DAY
OF HIS MARTYRDOM

**O Lord God, O Almighty, Father of your beloved and
blessed Son Jesus Christ, through whom we have received
the knowledge of you—God of angels and hosts and all creation—and of the whole race of saints who live under your
eyes!**

I bless you, because you have seen fit to bestow upon me this day and this hour, that I may share, among the number of the martyrs, the cup of your Anointed and rise to eternal life both in soul and in body, in virtue of the immortality of the Holy Spirit.
May I be accepted among them in your sight today as a rich and pleasing sacrifice, such as you, the true God that cannot utter a falsehood, have prearranged, revealed in advance, and now consummated.
And therefore I praise you for everything; I bless you, I glorify you through the eternal and heavenly High Priest Jesus Christ, your beloved Son, through whom be glory to you together with him and the Holy Spirit, both now and for the ages yet to come.
Amen.

THE SHEPHERD OF HERMAS

Visionary

Anyone who enjoys a good story would like **The Shepherd of Hermas**. It was very popular also among the early Fathers of the Church, especially St. Irenaeus, Origen, Tertullian and Clement of Alexandria. Written in dialogue form, the conversations are exchanges between Hermas and a woman who represents the Church and a young man who represents the angel of repentance. The latter is known as "the shepherd" from whom the title of the work is derived. Despite its narrative character, this work constitutes one of the essential means we have for discovering the theological and spiritual life of early Jewish Christianity.

Resembling the apocalyptic or visionary style found in St. John's **Revelation, The Shepherd of Hermas** is an exhortation to penance. It seems to have been written in several editions dating from as early as 90 A.D. Origen and Eusebius identify "Hermas" with the person mentioned in Romans 16:14, which would make it an apostolic work. Others, because the author mentions Clement of Rome, date it toward the end of the first century. A final conjecture, and perhaps the most correct, the "Muratorian Canon" indicates that it was probably written around 140-154 A.D.

The unknown author can be identified as having Jewish origins. That he is a simple, unaffected man of the people can be deduced from his casual comments about his relatives, his business, his farming, the defection of his children from the faith, his wife's talkativeness, and his own sins of thought about a woman other than his wife. His writing indicates that he was not an educated man but, rather, a single-minded person who intended to frighten evil people and to comfort the afflicted. His style, despite this purpose, remains lighthearted throughout.

The Shepherd of Hermas concerns itself chiefly with the dogma of the forgiveness of sins. Hermas introduces the teaching that in addition to the forgiveness of sins which occurred at baptism (adult baptism was in practice at the time), there was another single chance of forgiveness for one who was truly sorry. This idea was an advance over the previous one in the Church which declared that the baptismal forgiveness was the final one. However, Hermas' teaching does not seem to be of ecclesiastical origin nor is there proof for such a practice in Sacred Scripture. Nevertheless, the law in the Eastern Church followed his view until the fourth century, and in the west it was followed until the fifth century.

In regard to penitential practices, Hermas makes a distinction between "conversion" which he says is the work of the sinner and the "cure" which is the gift of God. His theme of the two paths, that of righteousness and that of unrighteousness, and his comparison of the good and bad angels as well as other similar comparisons, remind us of the "two ways" theme found in the **Didache**. And it is in **The Shepherd of Hermas** that we find the most ancient patristic references to the "Name" of Jesus seen as an efficacious reality in itself. Hermas declares, "To receive the Name of the Son of God" is "to escape death and give way to life." Elsewhere he adds, "No one can enter the Kingdom of God except through the Name of the Son," and, "The Name of the Son of God is great and immense; this is what supports the entire world."

The entire work of Hermas is divided into three broad sections: the VISIONS which depict the Church as a venerable old lady progressively growing younger as the visions proceed, indicating that she is moving from the state of a sinful people to that of the elect; the twelve MANDATES which require belief in various doctrines and virtues; and the ten PARABLES which are similar to the mandates but which give Christian examples, through pictorial, symbolic form, of how to live out these laws. A few examples from each section demonstrate the author's directness in approach:

VISIONS — Hermas, do not hold a grudge against your children...for a grudge is the worker of death...Hermas, cease saying all these prayers for your sins. Ask also for righteousness in order that you may take some of it to your household. ...Just as the round stone cannot be made square, unless it be cut and lose something, so also the rich in this world cannot be made useful for the Lord unless their riches have been cut out of them.

MANDATES — There are no beaten tracks on the crooked path. Instead, there is nothing but waste lands and numerous obstacles; it is rough and full of thorns. ...The Lord dwells amid long-suffering, but the devil has his abode in anger. ...Divided purpose is the daughter of the devil and exceedingly wicked to the servants of God.

PARABLES — The poor make intercession—these are their riches—and give back to the Lord who supplied them; in the same way the rich unhesitatingly put the riches they received from the Lord at the disposal of the poor. This is a great and acceptable work in the sight of God. ...Act as follows: after having done what is prescribed, on the day of your fast do not taste anything except bread and water. Compute the total expense for the food you would have eaten on the day on which you intended to keep a fast and give it to a widow, an orphan, or someone in need.

And for those who want God to answer their prayers, the Shepherd gives this message to Hermas, and through him to us:

Clothe yourself with cheerfulness, which always finds favor and acceptance from God. Rejoice in it, for every

cheerful person does good, has good thoughts, and despises sadness. On the other hand, the sad person is always committing sin. In the first place, they sin because they bring sadness to the Holy Spirit that was given to them as a spirit of gladness. In the second place, by bringing sadness to the Holy Spirit they commit grave sin because they do not intercede with God nor confess to God. Why does not the prayer of the sad person reach up to the altar of God? Because sadness resides in their hearts. Consequently, sadness mingled with their conversation does not let their prayer ascend clean to the altar. Just as vinegar mixed with wine in the same vessel does not have the same agreeable taste, so also sadness, associated with the Holy Spirit, has not the same power of impenetration. Cleanse yourself, then, of this wicked sadness and you will live to God. So, also, will all others live to God who cast away sadness and clothe themselves in complete cheerfulness.

JUSTIN MARTYR

Bridge Builder

Parents frustrated over children who dislike school or who do not appreciate the efforts they make to provide an education for them might consider asking St. Justin Martyr to intercede for them. This saint was born in Samaria sometime between 100-110 A.D. His parents were pagans, his father probably being a Roman. Very little is known about his early life other than the information we get from his own writings, chiefly in his **Dialogue With Trypho**.

From this work we learn that he was interested in and dabbled in the various philosophies of his day. He tells us he left the Stoic school of thought because it did not give him any explanation concerning God's being. Then he tried the school of a Peripatetic (one of the followers of Aristotle). When required to pay his tuition immediately upon entrance, he responded by not attending the lectures. Finally, he left the Pythagorean school because its prerequisites for the study of philosophy were music, astronomy and geometry. Though he dearly loved philosophy, he had no inclination toward any of these!

The stamina of the early Christian martyrs played a role in Justin's conversion: "...as I saw that they showed no fear in the face of death and of all other things which inspire horror, I reflected that they could not be vicious and pleasure-loving." But it was his insatiable search for truth which finally made him capitulate to Christ: "...the perception of immaterial things quite overpowered me, and the contemplation of ideas furnished my mind with wings..."

Justin found Platonic thought the most to his liking until one day, he tells us, as he walked along the beach, he met an aged Christian. This old man convinced him that Platonic philosophy could not satisfy the longing of his heart. To Justin's consternation at not knowing to whom he might turn for learning truth, the old man suggested he might study the prophets, saying, "These alone both saw and announced the truth to us, neither reverencing nor fearing any one, not influenced by a desire for glory." About this encounter, Justin wrote further:

...straightway a flame was kindled in my soul, and a love of the prophets and of all those who are friends of Christ possessed me; while revolving his words in my mind, I found this philosophy alone to be safe and profitable. Thus and for this reason I became a philosopher. Moreover I wish that everyone making a similar resolution to my own would not turn away from the words of the Savior (Dial. 8).

His passion for truth not only converted Justin, but it also formed the base of his life's work, the defense of the Christian faith. For this reason he was known as an "apologist," one who defends the faith. His biography even gives evidence to his step by step apologetical style or approach. He used to travel about as an itinerant teacher wearing the *pallium*, a cloak worn by Greek philosophers, as if to indicate that he had found the true philosophy above all others. Today we would probably say it was to show his continuity with tradition or the past.

It is believed that after his numerous travels he finally reached Rome where he founded a school. Because he was the first Church writer who tried through his systematic presentation of Christian truth to bridge the gap between Christianity and pagan philosophy, some scholars call him the founder of theological literature. He was convinced "that everyone who can speak the truth and does not speak it shall be judged by God."

During the life of Justin, Christians were often charged with atheism because they refused to worship pagan gods. One of the saint's chief aims as an apologist was to obtain justice for these Christians. He extolled their high moral code which made them good citizens. Despite the debt of gratitude the world would later owe to Justin for his effort to reconcile Christian and pagan cultures, he was misunderstood both by his own Christian contemporaries and by the civil rulers. He was beheaded in Rome probably around 165 A.D. during the reign of Marcus Aurelius.

In addition to his **Dialogue With Trypho**, only two **Apologies** (usually considered one work) have been preserved from Justin's writings. In them we find some of his most profound thought. He was the first Christian author to contrast Mary and Eve. According to Justin, Eve, a virgin, conceived the word of the serpent and brought forth disobedience and death. In contrast, Mary, a virgin, conceived the Word of God and brought forth Christ who destroyed both the serpent and death.

We find that the ancient liturgies described by Justin are similar to our own. Regarding the Eucharist, he says there should be a reading from the Gospel or prophets, a prayer, the kiss of peace, an offertory, prayers of consecration and the distribution of Communion. He points out that the people should be given the opportunity to express their assent to the liturgy at the conclusion of the prayers and thanksgiving by a hearty, "Amen!" Finally, he speaks of the parish custom of taking up a collection for the poor. He describes baptism as that event which takes us from the state of being children of necessity and ignorance to that of being children of choice and knowledge.

Justin, always in awe of the marvels of nature, defends the resurrection by declaring that it is not any more incredible than human birth:

Because you have never seen a dead person rise, you disbelieve. But just as in the beginning you would not have believed that from a little drop such persons might be produced, and yet you see them so produced, so now in the same way realize that it is not impossible for human bodies, after they have been put into the earth like seeds

and dissolved into death, to rise again in God's appointed time and put on incorruption (from the First Apology).

Regarding his life as a Christian, Justin tells us how he experienced his life by referring to the words of Christ. He asserts the words of Christ, "...possess a terrible power in themselves, and are sufficient to inspire with awe those who turn aside from the path of rectitude, while the sweetest rest is afforded those who make a diligent practice of them." He adds, "If, then, you have any concern for yourself, and if you are eagerly looking for salvation, and if you believe in God, you may—since you are not indifferent to the matter—become acquainted with the Christ of God, and after being initiated, live a happy life" (Dial. 8).

IRENAEUS

The Glory of God:
People Fully Alive!

Though St. Justin was perhaps the greatest Greek apologist of the second century, St. Irenaeus was its most important theologian. This talented, gifted man of God was born in Asia Minor. Scholars conjecture about the date of his birth—any time between 120 and 160 A.D.—but most place his death at the beginning of the third century. His home town was probably Smyrna. Historians come to this conclusion because as a boy he visited St. Polycarp. In a letter to Florinus, a Roman presbyter, Irenaeus wrote:

> **For, when I was still a boy, I knew you (Florinus) in lower Asia, in Polycarp's house...I remember the events of those days more clearly than those which happened recently, for what we learn as children grows up with the soul and is united to it, so that I can speak even of the place in which blessed Polycarp sat and disputed, how he came in and went out, the character of his life, the appearance of his body, the discourses which he made to the people, how he reported his intercourse with John and with the others who had seen the Lord...**

Such closeness to Polycarp put Irenaeus in touch with the Apostolic age even though, strictly speaking, he is not listed among the Apostolic Fathers. Why he left Asia Minor and went

THE GLORY
OF GOD
IS EACH PERSON
FULLY ALIVE!

IRENAEUS

to Gaul is unknown, as are the circumstances of his ordination. At any rate, there is evidence that he succeeded Pothinus as bishop of Lyons around the year 177 A.D. Tradition claims he died, possibly as a martyr, during the early years of the third century.

Despite lack of knowledge regarding the external events of his life, Irenaeus has the reputation of being the founder of Christian theology as we know it today. Those who dispute this claim do so only because they argue that Irenaeus' works are catechetical rather than theological in nature. His most important work, **Against Heresies**, is concerned chiefly with a refutation of the Gnostic and Montanist heresies. The Gnostics claimed they possessed secret knowledge not given to the rest of humankind. The Montanists claimed that the "just" God of the Old Testament and the "good" God of the New Testament were two separate deities. It was Irenaeus' task to place emphasis on the Church as the interpreter of doctrine and to identify the God of the Old and New Testaments as one and the same God.

In fulfilling this task, his unique teaching on Christology turned out to be his most famous achievement in the area of doctrine. Christ, for Irenaeus, was the "treasure hidden in the field." He was the *Logos* (the Word), the complete revelation of the Father's love. He summed up all creation; he was its beginning and its end, the *Alpha* and *Omega*. He was the second Adam who restored to humans the position lost by the original fall. This idea of Christ restoring all things from the beginning and for all time is called Irenaeus' doctrine of "recapitulation"—that is, Christ takes up and redeems all of creation in himself. According to him, Christ enables humans to fulfill all their potentialities for perfection and immortality. In his words, frequently quoted, "God became human so that humans might become God." Refreshingly modern, he viewed this "becoming" as developmental—a gradual process by which humans become "accustomed" to the ways of God. Because his theology is so rooted in the relationship of Christ with creation, especially with the human race, it is termed *incarnational*.

Irenaeus described Christ's taking flesh of the Virgin Mary by the Holy Spirit as a way of "renovating" us. In his writings, he refers again and again to this capacity of humans to be "created again after the image and likeness of God." He stresses that the whole work of salvation is to "receive again in Christ Jesus what we had lost in Adam—that is, the image and likeness of God." This ancient Father, modern as any current theologian, focused attention on the risen Jesus and on our resurrection. We are glorified in Christ; or to put it in his own words, "The glory of God is the human person fully alive, and the human person's life is to see God."

In a letter written by some of the martyrs of Lyons which recommends Irenaeus to the pope, we see the high esteem accorded to him by the people of his own diocese. His name comes from the Greek word, *peace*.* Irenaeus lived up to his name, especially on one occasion when a dispute arose between Pope Victor and some of his bishops. It seems liturgical discontent was not confined to our own day, for the dispute arose over, of all things, the date Easter should be celebrated! In Irenaeus' time the eastern Christians were following the date of the Jewish Passover while those in the west observed it on Sunday. The quarrel resulted in the excommunication of the eastern bishops and Irenaeus was moved by the Spirit to write to the pope in a spirit of pacification. His efforts were successful and years later the easterners, on their own, adjusted their calendar to the practice of having Easter celebrated on Sunday.

Though very learned, Irenaeus did not claim to be a great writer. About this he says, "You will not expect from me, who am resident among the Celts and am accustomed for the most part to use a barbarous dialect, any display of rhetoric, which I have never learned, or any excellence of composition which I have never practiced, or any beauty and persuasiveness of style, to which I make no pretensions. But you will accept in a kindly spirit what I in a like spirit write to you simply, truthfully, and in my own homely way." He could also say, "It is better and more useful for a man to know little or nothing, while coming near to God

---

*A point of interest here to those who bear the name **Irene** is that, paradoxically, the preface of his name, "ire" often denotes just the opposite quality as, for example, when one's "ire" has been raised.

through love, than to imagine that he knows much and has gained many experiences, and yet to be found a blasphemer and an enemy of God." Nevertheless, it was Irenaeus' opinion that ignorance breeds fear and it was with the hope of dispelling some of this ignorance that he set himself to the task of writing, despite his misgivings about his abilities.

In one of his finest passages, Irenaeus describes, in a characteristically modern thought pattern, the evolutionary progression of the Eucharist toward its end, the resurrection of our bodies and thus, ultimately, toward the resurrection of the whole Body of Christ. The passage exemplifies how deeply this man's incarnational view was bound up with earthly realities:

> **In the fashion in which life's root, placed in the ground, produces fruit in due time, and the seed cast upon the ground and decomposed, reappears multiplied by the Spirit of God which is in all things, and then those elements which in God's wisdom come to be used by man, receiving the Word of God, become Eucharist in the body and blood of Christ, so also our bodies nourished by this Eucharist, committed to the earth and there decomposed, will rise in time because the Word of God will make them rise for the glory of God the Father.**

One wonders if any better proof of the resurrection of our bodies has been written by authors since Irenaeus wrote these words. He is truly a man for our day!

CLEMENT OF ALEXANDRIA

Out of the Ghetto

Clement of Alexandria was born, probably in Athens, while St. Polycarp was still living and Sts. Justin and Ignatius were in their prime. The date usually given by scholars is 150 A.D. Some speculate he might have met some acquaintances of Ignatius, Polycarp, or even of St. John while he was in Alexandria. All agree he writes as though he had first-hand knowledge of the apostolic tradition.

Clement's birth into a pagan family is surmised from the fact that he was well acquainted with Greek pagan customs, rites and literature, though there is some disagreement among historians as to when he became a Christian. Some say he converted only while he, as was customary among people of his time, traveled around in search of a broader education; others say, rather, that Clement shows a very early familiarity with Christianity. Since it was such a quiet event, some have supposed that he must have had neither great sins nor was a great renunciation involved in this step for him. One thing is certain: it is our misfortune not to know what went on in his heart at the moment of his conversion.

He traveled to southern Italy, Syria and Palestine and finally to Alexandria around 180 A.D. where he found Pantaenus, Christian founder of the famous catechetical school in that city. Of his well-loved teacher Clement wrote: "He, the true Sicilian bee, gathering the spoil of the flowers of the prophetic and apostolic meadows, engendered in the souls of his hearers a deathless element of knowledge." Christianity had already undergone some evangelical work in Alexandria through the efforts of Philo the Jew whose neo-Platonic thought had left its imprint. This liberal and humanistic thought suited Clement's temperament and convictions. The school itself, something like a modern study club, was the beginning of our contemporary Christian university. In Clement's time, the school was private, neither originated by nor directed by ecclesiastical authority. Its students were Alexandrian Greeks— pagan and Christian men and women of the well-to-do class. Though elementary lessons of Christianity were taught, the emphasis was chiefly on Sacred Scripture.

Succeeding Pantaenus as teacher of the school, Clement was soon forced by the persecution of Septimius Severus to flee to Cappadocia where he took refuge with his pupil Alexander, later bishop of Jerusalem. Tradition holds that Clement suffered martyrdom around 215 A.D. For a long time counted among the "blessed fathers" and venerated as a saint, he was never officially canonized because of his association with the Alexandrian school, considered "tainted" with the teachings of Origen. Actually, though Origen was Clement's most famous pupil and succeeded the latter as head of the school, the two teachers differed greatly both in doctrine and in methodology.

Alexander spoke of Clement as "my teacher, who was to me so greatly useful and helpful." Nor was he the only one to praise him. St. Cyril of Alexandria called him "a man admirably learned and skillful and one that searched to the depths all the learning of the Greeks within an exactness rarely attained before." St. Jerome pronounced him the most learned of all the ancients, though not all scholars would accord him this superlative. Clement was, however, considered one of the founders of Christian literature. One author called him the "pioneer of Christian scholarship."

Knowledgeable in diverse subjects—philosophy, poetry, archaeology, mythology, literature—Clement, in his writings, quotes frequently from Scripture and the Greek classics. He interpreted Sacred Scripture allegorically in the fashion of Philo and calls on

Homer, Plato and the best writers of Greece to substantiate his arguments. He was shrewd enough to recognize that the Church could not avoid competing with pagan philosophy and literature if she were to fulfill her obligation to humankind as the teacher of the nations.

If in St. Justin we had one of the first Fathers who tried to reconcile the Christian faith with Hellenic thought, Clement went further. In him we find Christianity facing a different culture for the first time. We might call him the first "ecumenist"; he met non-Christians on their own terms. He proved that the Gospel and secular learning, faith and philosophy, are not enemies but belong together if Christians are to live in a real world. Unlike his pupil Origen, Clement was not a disciplined thinker. Uncomfortable with logic, he was more interested in winning hearts than in crushing the opposition. Indeed, it is this very "fault," if such it be, of seeking ways to reconcile irreconcilable traditional and contemporary ideas that has led some to call him the first "speculative theologian."

In opposing the evils of his day Clement did not demand that Christians renounce all the refinements of their culture. Instead, he worked on attitudes. In the matter of poverty, for example, he advocated restriction of conveniences and luxuries on the part of Christians so as to allow them to be independent of material things and free for others. He pointed out that if all Christians gave up their possessions, there would no longer be the possibility of supporting the poor. For him it was crucial, rather, that the salt of Christianity permeate the whole of society. In regard to evil, he further suggests that fear of the Lord is good even

> **...if bitter. Sick, we truly stand in the need of the Saviour; having wandered, of one to guide us; blind, of one to lead us to light; thirsty, of the fountain of life of which whosoever partakes shall no longer thirst; dead, we need life; sheep, we need a shepherd; we who are children need a tutor while universal humanity stands in need of Jesus (Paedagogus I, 9).**

WRITINGS

Clement's three best-known works, still in existence, are **Protrepticus** ("An Exhortation to the Greeks"), **Paedagogus** (literally, "leader of children," or, as has been titled, "The Educator" or "Tutor"), and **Stromata** (literally, "scatter rugs" or "carpets," or, as we would express it, "miscellaneous"). In his **Protrepticus**, he intended to arouse the enthusiasm of the Greeks for Christ. Like the early apologists, he appealed to them to convert, to recognize that all the truth and beauty of the philosophers and poets could be found in the "New Song," Christ, who could fulfill all human desire. In this work we see Clement the contemplative and the sublime poet preferring to speak of the beauties of truth rather than to argue its existence.

In **Paedagogus,** his most famous work, Clement continues his exhortation to the Greeks. It is made up of two books. The first discusses the person and the educational function of Christ as instructor, and the second, which exhorts readers to transform their personal and social lives through right living, deals with problems of daily life down to the minutest detail. The topics—dress, eating, drinking, dancing, bathing, sleeping—give us an interesting description of the kind of luxury and vice prevalent in Alexandria at the time. He even discusses such things as music and furniture.

The **Stromata** allows Clement to be light and entertaining in presentation—a literary form favored by the philosophers of his day. He wrote of various topics at random, weaving them together like a patchwork quilt. In eight books of this work he deals with the relationship of the Christian religion with secular learning. The other books deal with his refutation of Gnosticism. Characteristically, Clement does not denounce the heresy which held that faith and knowledge were in contradiction. He points out, instead, that a harmony of faith and knowledge is not only possible but that together they produce true "gnosis" or knowledge, and declares that Christ, the *Logos*, the Word, is the highest religious explanation of the world.

DEVELOPMENT OF CLEMENT'S DOCTRINE

Doctrinally, Clement wrote on numerous subjects. He saw the Church as a virgin mother "...and calling her children to her she nurses them with holy milk, the *Logos*," and the "school in which Jesus is the teacher." In this connection, he calls Christians "graduates of his blessed tutorship." He spoke of the hierarchy consisting in three grades: episcopacy, priesthood, diaconate—comparing this order to the hierarchy of the angels, a comparison which introduced a new development in the theology of the angels.

Though he praised virginity in those to whom "God has given this," and practiced it himself, he seemed to regard matrimony as superior to the virginal life when comparing the two. Because there is little evidence that his opinion was held by any other Church Father, it has been suggested that his emphasis was the result of his eagerness to defend marriage against the Gnostics who discredited it. He goes so far as to say, "Therefore we must by all means marry, both for our country's sake, for the succession of children and as far as we are concerned for the perfection of the world." Nevertheless, at least in some respects, Clement's lofty view of matrimony might be of help to those whose marriages are faltering today. He emphasized that a true marriage was beyond sexual union, that it was a "sacred state," a spiritual and religious union. In fact, he was so strong in the opinion that this union continued forever that he did not favor a second marriage after the death of one's partner.

He spoke of Baptism as a rebirth and regeneration and of us as adopted children of God, originating such terms as "seal," "illumination," and "bath" in regard to this sacrament. About the Eucharist he said, "And to drink the blood of Jesus, is to become partaker of the Lord's immortality—the Spirit being the energetic principle of the Word as the blood is of the flesh." He taught that the Sacrament of Reconciliation could be received only twice—once preceding Baptism and then, "out of mercy for human weakness," once more for all sins except that of turning away from God and refusing reconciliation.

Perhaps in our tense, ever-changing society we learn a lesson from Clement. He was able to take the risk of making a few mistakes at times for the cause of truth. May we also tenaciously cling only to God who is true while having the gracious willingness to modify the way we express our long-held beliefs so that doctrines of the faith will appeal to a world rapidly moving into the twenty-first century.

> **This One who is from David and before David**
> **This Word of God, looking beyond lyre and harp,**
> **mindless instruments,**
> **By his Holy Spirit tunes the Cosmos,**
> **Especially this little cosmos, the human person,**
> **mind and body;**
> **And he sings to God with this many-voiced instrument—**
> **He accompanies his song with the instrument**
> **of the human person.**
>
> **(Clement of Alexandria—**
> **EXHORTATION TO THE HEATHEN)**

What then does this instrument, the Word of God, the Lord, the New Song desire? To open the eyes of the blind and unstop the ears of the deaf; to lead the lame or the erring to righteousness; to exhibit God to the foolish; to put a stop to corruption; to conquer death; to reconcile disobedient children to their Father.

> **(Clement of Alexandria—**
> **EXHORTATION TO THE HEATHEN)**

PERPETUA

Peaceful Protester

Our contemporary protest movements had their counterparts in early Christianity. Though we have very little information about the life of Perpetua, we do have an authentic account of the amazing acts of protest which were accomplished by her in the very early years of the third century. Accounts of the early Christian martyrs are often fictional embellishments of what really took place. **The Martyrdom of Perpetua** is a rare exception to this rule.

During the persecution by Septimus Severus in 202-203 A.D. six friends were arrested in Carthage, Africa: Vibia Perpetua, leader of the group; her slave, Felicitas, eight months pregnant; Saturus, already a Christian and the instructor of the others; Revocatus, Saturninus, and Secundulus, three catechumens. After their baptism the new converts were closely watched by the authorities and all were jailed a few days later. Perpetua asserts that, at the time of her baptism "the Spirit instructed me not to request anything from the baptismal waters except endurance of physical suffering" (**The Martyrdom of Perpetua**, #3). While waiting for her death sentence to take place, Perpetua's relatives—a mother, two brothers and an aunt—pleaded with her, for the sake of her aged father and for her baby whom she was still nursing, to give up her new faith. All to no avail.

The account of Perpetua's death is one of the earliest descriptions we have of the high regard the early Church had for martyrdom. It was seen as the supreme symbol of human liberation and self-fulfillment. And in our own day when we hear of many so-called "apocalyptic" events, the accounts of the death of martyrs can be said to be truly apocalyptic, especially if we consider the visions they experienced before death. Perpetua, too, had her visions. They assured her she would not be freed and that she would be victorious as a martyr. The events that followed proved her prophecy true. The accounts of Christian martyrdom given in later centuries are, in their recounting of events, largely dependent on that of Perpetua.

In addition to establishing the symbolic value of martyrdom **The Martyrdom of Perpetua** is valuable and unique in other ways. It gives us an idea of the vitality of the early Church in northern Africa. It is a narrative which is told by two people who were actually involved in the events as well as by an outside witness who comments on them (some have suggested that in this case it might have been Tertullian). This is a rarity among historical documents, that is, to have the testimony of those who were participants in the events combined with the testimony of someone who later verifies them. Rarer still is that part of the account was written by a woman. It is, in fact, the earliest of such writings in Christian literature.

Consequently we are presented with a feminine viewpoint and are given an insight into the status of women of her day. We find that women enjoyed an equality in leadership roles with men unknown in later periods of Christianity. In fact, the feminine/masculine characteristics which make up each human being are found in the terms used to describe Perpetua at different moments: **bride, mother, sister, daughter, lady** as well as **leader, warrior, victor, fighter**. Finally, though we have almost no historical facts about the life of Perpetua the account gives us a graphic look at the personality of this courageous woman who was about twenty years old when she made the supreme sacrifice of her life for Jesus.

Like ourselves, people of Perpetua's time regarded non-violent protest as a legitimate form of disobedience and disrespect of societal norms and customs. The martyrs saw God's law as superseding any laws established by society. The certainty of the end times and of another life only encouraged them further to defy any human loyalty or any form of punishment, however painful. They saw death as the beginning of fulfillment of their existence. Amazingly, throughout **The Martyrdom of Perpetua** we find a woman who exhibits deep concern for others despite the desperateness of her own immediate life and death situation.

How do we see this exemplified? One of the greatest sufferings Perpetua endured while in prison was her inability to relieve the anxiety her imprisonment caused her parents and siblings: "I suffered intensely because I sensed their agony on my account" (ibid., #3). An equal, if not greater suffering was her worry over the health and safety of her young child. For a short while she was allowed to have him with her in prison and during that time she was relieved of her anxiety and concern, but shortly before her martyrdom the child was given to her father who refused to return him to her. Perpetua remained undaunted, however, and saw this as providential, saying, "Then God saw to it that my child no longer needed my nursing, nor were my breasts inflamed" (ibid., #3). For her, ultimately, civil or familial disobedience became a matter of affirming the reality of the yet to come over the reality of the here and now.

At one point during her imprisonment, Perpetua's brother persuaded her to ask God for a vision to discover if she would be condemned or freed. In her vision she saw a very narrow bronze ladder reaching to heaven. Her teacher, Saturus, went up first. When he arrived at the top he looked back and told her he was waiting for her and warned her not to be bitten by the dragon which was below. Perpetua continues the account:

I told him that in the name of Jesus Christ the dragon could not harm me. At this the dragon slowly lowered its head as though afraid of me. Using its head as the first step I began my ascent (ibid., #4).

For her the message was clear: she was not to be freed from prison but she would win the victory of a martyr's death.

The day before she was to go into the arena she had another vision in which she was confronted, not by beasts, but by an

Egyptian "horrible to look at, accompanied by fighters who were to help defeat me" (ibid., #10). However, there were also some young men present who had been sent to help and encourage her. As her opponent tried to grab her feet, she says, "I felt myself being lifted up into the air and began to strike at him as one who was no longer earth-bound" (ibid., #10). She took his head between her hands and pushed. As his head hit the ground, she stepped on it in victory, the scene similar to the one in which she confronted the dragon. She realized through this vision that she would be contending, not with the wild beasts, but with Evil itself.

The martyrdom of Perpetua is incomplete without mentioning the courageous witness of her companion in suffering, Felicitas, who, when these events took place, was eight months pregnant. Because the law would not allow the execution of pregnant women, Felicitas was distressed that her martyrdom might be delayed and that she would not be able to die with her friends. She and the other prisoners prayed to God that her baby would be born prematurely. Her labor pains began and, after the birth of a little girl she gave the child to one of her sisters to raise, rejoicing now that she could join her companions in the arena.

Before the day of the public games, the prisoners were treated with unusual severity by the commanding officer because it had been suggested that they might escape through some trickery. Perpetua challenged him: "Why don't you at least allow us to freshen up, the most noble of the condemned, since we belong to Caesar and are about to fight on his birthday? Or isn't it to your credit that we should appear in good condition on that day?" (ibid., #16). The officer blushed and ordered them to be treated more kindly. Even the warden had become a believer by this time.

The prisoners tried to make their last meal together as much of an "agape" as possible. The final events as provided by the commentator are worth quoting in greater detail:

> **The day of their victory dawned, and with joyful counte-nances they marched from the prison to the arena as though on their way to heaven. If there was any trembling it was from joy, not fear. Perpetua followed with quick**

step as a true spouse of Christ, the darling of God, her brightly flashing eyes quelling the gaze of the crowd. Felicitas too, joyful because she had safely survived childbirth and was now able to participate in the contest with the wild animals, passed from one shedding of blood to another; from midwife to gladiator, about to be purified after childbirth by a second baptism. As they were led through the gate they were ordered to put on different clothes. ... But that noble woman stubbornly resisted to the end. She said, "We've come this far voluntarily in order to protect our rights, and we've pledged our lives not to recapitulate on any such matter as this. We made this agreement with you." Injustice bowed to justice and the guard conceded that they could enter the arena in their ordinary dress. Perpetua was singing victory psalms as if already crushing the head of the Egyptian (ibid., #18).

The account goes on to say that the martyrs were given the "instrument of torture" they wished, that is, the kind of animals they were to fight with—leopards, bears and so on—or whether they were to be confronted with one or several animals. As for Perpetua and Felicitas, it is recorded:

For the young women the devil had readied a mad cow, an animal not usually used at these games, but selected so that the women's sex would be matched with that of the animal. After being stripped and enmeshed in nets, the women were led into the arena. How horrified the people were as they saw that one was a young girl and the other, her breasts dripping with milk, had just recently given birth to a child. Consequently both were recalled and dressed in loosely fitting gowns.

Perpetua was tossed first and fell on her back. She sat up, and being more concerned with her sense of modesty than her pain, covered her thighs with her gown which had been torn down one side. Then finding her hair-clip

**which had fallen out, she pinned back her loose hair
thinking it not proper for a martyr to suffer with dishev-
elled hair; it might seem that she was mourning in her
hour of triumph. Then she stood up. Noticing that
Felicitas was badly bruised, she went to her, reached out
her hands and helped her to her feet (ibid., #20).**

How touching to note the feminine details expressed in these
passages! After the above incident, Perpetua seemed to have
gone into a trance and was not aware that she had already been
engaged in combat. She asked, "When are we going to be led
out to that cow, or whatever it is?" (ibid., #20). The account tells
us that she would not believe that it had already happened until
she saw the blood stains on her body and clothing.

Even at that moment she exhorted her brother and one of
the catechumens, "Remain strong in your faith and love one
another. Do not let our excruciating sufferings become a stum-
bling block for you" (ibid., #20). It was the custom that if the
beasts did not actually kill them in the arena, the prisoners were
dispatched by the soldiers afterward with a sword. In this contest, all the prisoners were still living after their encounter with
the animals. The crowd clamored to have them brought out in
the open so they could see them finished off with the sword.
The witness who finished the narrative added a rather poignant
liturgical comment: "...they voluntarily arose and moved where
the crowd wanted them. Before doing so they kissed each other
so that their martyrdom would be completely perfected by the
rite of the kiss of peace" (ibid., #21).

Saturus preceded the other martyrs in death so as to be the
first to climb the ladder and to be Perpetua's encouragement as
had been predicted. When it was her turn, "...in order to feel
some of the pain, groaning as she was struck between the ribs,
she took the gladiator's trembling hand and guided it to her
throat" (ibid., #21). The writer of the account closes by making
this observation: "Perhaps it was that so great a woman, feared
as she was by the unclean spirit, could not have been slain had
she not herself willed it" (ibid., #21).

TERTULLIAN

The Firebrand

Those who have trouble practicing the virtue of patience may find a companion spirit in Tertullian, a kind of "all or nothing at all" Christian. This early Church Father wrote a treatise on the subject, remarking that he felt like an invalid speaking on the topic of health for, as he candidly admitted, he was always sick with the fever of impatience. St. Jerome, often titled "the irascible" himself, once said that Tertullian was "a man always on fire." What were the external circumstances surrounding the life of this firebrand? Do they give us a clue as to why he developed such an impetuous spirit?

Born of pagan parents in Carthage (near the area of modern Tunisia) around 155 A.D., Tertullian spent his earliest years in this city colonized by the Romans. Later on, his father, a centurion, sent him to Rome where he studied law and rhetoric, two disciplines which he later used to advantage in explaining his beliefs. Though he claimed he led a dissolute life in Rome, it was there also that he converted to Christianity. Eventually he married, but whether or not he was a priest is disputed by historians. St. Jerome said he was, but the strongest evidence of historians seems to indicate that he was not. Upon the completion of his education, he returned to Carthage where he practiced law.

Tertullian never recorded for us why he became a Christian, but the reason inferred by some is that he, like Justin before him, was inspired by the courage of Christian martyrs who faced torture and death with such fortitude. Other historians believed the teachings of Christianity had an appeal for his uncompromising nature since these required its adherents to make an ultimate decision for Christ. Still others credit both factors as having some bearing on his conversion. Such speculations do seem credible, especially the first, for, years later, he left the Church to follow the Montanists, a sect which advocated martyrdom. In his own writings Tertullian argued that martyrdom was simply carrying Christian opposition to idolatry to its logical conclusion. Since this opposition was a matter of life or death, martyrdom was a duty! It is ironic, therefore, that he lived to feeble old age, not dying until around 220 A.D.

With such a background, why is Tertullian, who died outside the Church, considered one of its great Fathers? It must be admitted that the Church, in his time, was less sophisticated regarding its pronouncements on what constituted heresy and what did not. In fact the Montanists had not been declared heretical at the time Tertullian joined the group. Further, he was attracted to them for a most religious reason: he saw in them the living spirit of early Christianity. They were enthusiastic and stressed renewal of life and repentance for one's sins; their morality far surpassed that of most of his contemporaries. Though history obscures the end of his life from us, it seems that he broke off from the Montanists before he died and founded his own sect. There is some indication that Augustine discovered this group around the fourth century and converted them. If so, then we might like to think of Tertullian as being exonerated by proxy through his followers.

What does the Church owe Tertullian? With the exception of Augustine, many historians would classify him as the most important thinker of the West in the period preceding the Council of Nicea (325 A.D.). Though the people of Carthage and the surrounding area were Greek in culture, they spoke Latin. Tertullian translated the theology of the time into their own language and, by so doing, became the first western theologian. He was also the only theologian whose works—even those of his Montanist period—have survived the centuries intact. He is considered the most original and penetrating interpreter of Sacred Scripture of his time because he had a realization of and emphasized its unique character. He was the one who formulated the first formal teaching of the Church we have on original sin, namely, that it stemmed from Adam.

Tertullian was the most prolific Latin writer before the time of Constantine. His works can be divided into his pre- and post-Montanist periods, though it is not always certain to which period each work belongs. Of the thirty-one treatises still in existence, his largest and most important work for the Church was that which contained five books refuting the Marcionists. Ten treatises dealt with dogmatic teachings in which he was the first to claim that the Church is the possessor of faith and the Scriptures and therefore has the right to decide on the scope and content of faith.

He also wrote five works on apologetics. In these he capitalized on his abilities as a lawyer to win advantages for the Christians of his day. We might even compare him to modern champions of human rights. Combining his talents of clarity in thought with his literary skill he argued in his **Apology** that the persecution of Christians was illegal because it denied them their rights as citizens. He declared that while other criminals were allowed a defense, Christian "criminals" were not and that torture was applied to others in order to obtain a confession while Christians were tortured in order to obtain a denial.

He had a passion for truth (in one work alone he used the term "truth" 162 times). Though impatient by nature he never lost his temper. Instead he became more polished and subtle as he wrote against any opposition to his ideas. He liked to startle readers with obscure facts. As a result, his writings sound like he is trying to win a case. In an effort to annihilate his adversaries, he always tried to prove too much and often ended up silencing them without convincing them. He did not seem capable of following his own axiom, "Truth persuades by teaching, but does not teach by persuading." And though thorough and orderly in thought, his skill in argumentation sometimes caused him to be carried away and inclined toward exaggeration in order to prove his point. One expert on the Fathers said all his writings were controversial and that he attacked the laxity of the Catholic

Church with as much vigor as he had once attacked the pagans. On the other hand, he always adapted his writings to his readers—whether simple catechumens or learned heretics—and though his works were scholarly, they were never dull.

All the rest of Tertullian's works dealt with practical and ascetical matters. In these he wrote on subjects ranging from the apparel of women to behavior during times of persecution. His innate Roman spirit made him interested in the real world. He always spoke in concrete terms and moved toward practical decisions not only in that world but in his own spiritual and intellectual world as well. His works on prayer, patience and repentance are the most important for us in reaching his inner spirit. In the following rather amusing passage from his work on patience we can detect his characteristic disciplined thought as well as this movement toward the practical order:

I will comment further on the pleasure of patience... The reason why anyone hurts you is that you may be pained, because the hurter's enjoyment consists in the pain of the hurt. When, then, you have upset his enjoyment by not being pained, he must needs be pained by the loss of his enjoyment. Then you not only go away unhurt, which alone is sufficient for you, but gratified in the bargain by your adversary's disappointment and revenged by his pain. This is the utility and the pleasure of patience (Of Patience, Ch. 8 ANF).

We might question how much the spirit of Christianity motivates this statement, but it does seem a good example of Tertullian trying to convince the reader through his own method of logic, that patience would be a good thing—even for himself! What things in the life and writings of Tertullian can Christians imitate? Though we may feel we would rather admire than imitate him, he does have something to teach us about dedication to our life goals and about the love of truth. He is also one of those straightforward persons who challenge us to leave our comfortable points of view and take a stance on matters that are important. We can thank him for that. The following short quotations indicate that Tertullian was also a man of depth and insight:

—We are not born Christians, but become such.

—The blood of martyrs is the seed of faith.

—It is prayer alone which vanquishes God.

—He (Christ) came to reform and enlighten our receptivity.

—God is an immensity of goodness...he is eager for our trust.

—That we may not be as far from the ears of God as we are from his precepts, the memory of his precepts paves for our prayers a way to heaven...

—Not merely from anger, but altogether from <u>all</u> perturbation of mind, ought the exercise of prayer to be free, uttered from a spirit such as the Spirit to whom it is sent. For a defiled spirit cannot be acknowledged by a holy spirit, nor a sad by a joyful, nor a fettered by a free.

—In proportion as you have no mercy on yourself, believe me, in just this same measure God will have mercy upon you.

Prayer alone is that which vanquishes God. Christ has willed that it be operative for no evil. ...It knows nothing save how to recall the souls of the departed from the very path of death, to transform the weak, to restore the sick, to purge the possessed, to open prison bars, to loose the bonds of the innocent. Likewise it washes away faults, repels temptations, extinguishes persecutions, consoles the fainthearted, cheers

the high-spirited, escorts travellers, appeases waves, makes
robbers stand aghast, nourishes the poor, governs the rich,
upraises the fallen, arrests the falling, confirms the standing.

(Tertullian—ON PRAYER)

Prayer is the wall of faith; her arms and missiles against the
foe who keeps watch over us on all sides. And, so never walk
we unarmed.

(Tertullian—ON PRAYER)

ORIGEN

The Man of Steel

Among the early Fathers, Origen was one of the most original thinkers in the Church. That is not simply a pun. Born in Egypt, his life span (c. 184-254 A.D.) made him a contemporary of St. Irenaeus of Lyons and St. Clement of Alexandria. Both his parents were Christian. His father, a devout man who gave him a liberal education and who taught him to memorize and to love Sacred Scripture, was martyred for the faith when Origen was only seventeen. His mother, fearing the young man might try to follow his father's example, hid his clothes to prevent him from leaving the house. History does not reveal to us why this particular deterrent proved to be so successful. At any rate, the death of his father left Origen with the responsibility of supporting his mother and six younger brothers.

Around 203 A.D., he was invited to teach at the catechetical school of Alexandria, succeeding St. Clement. His zeal for this work was so great that he sold all his secular books and all other teaching. It is said that he inspired his students to seek martyrdom and that some of them actually became martyrs. This was not unusual in Origen's time when simply to be a Christian was to invite death. Although it is not known whether he himself was a martyr, he did suffer imprisonment and torture during the persecution of Decius, who became emperor in 249 A.D.

Because of a certain unfortunate rivalry between the priests and the *didaskalos* or lay teachers, Origen's life did not always run smoothly. In order to be able to function more efficiently, he accepted ordination outside his own diocese and from a bishop other than his own. Consequently, he incurred the displeasure of his own bishop and was expelled from Alexandria. For this and other reasons, he became a controversial figure in his own day and for several subsequent centuries in the Church.

To his contemporaries he was a sign of contradiction. He was one of the most widely-traveled persons of the time and an intellectual. At the same time he was a seeker of the crucified Christ, living a life of extreme austerity and self-denial. He practiced celibacy, fasted, slept on the ground and gave his energies, both day and night, to much study, especially of the Scriptures. Naturally, his asceticism caused him difficulties with others who could not understand such a manner of life. It was perhaps one of the reasons his bishop had refused him ordination. Nevertheless, some scholars hold that his life-style became the basis for what is known today as monastic life.

The combination of both secular and religious thought given to him by his father prepared Origen to develop the most successful synthesis of pagan Hellenism and Christianity found in the third century. He harmoniously blended Scripture, philosophy and poetry with incredible ease. No doubt these inclinations and abilities partially account for the fact that he was much in demand as a speaker in different countries.

Though not the best, Origen was the most prolific writer of the early Church. Because he gave most of his attention to the ideas he wrote about, he was less careful about his style than some of the Fathers. In spite of this, he was dubiously dubbed "the man of steel" because of his great tenacity in composing such a vast amount of work. Many of his writings have been lost simply because there were so many of them. Others perished because the hastiness with which he formulated his ideas cost him the censure of Church authorities.

WORKS OF ORIGEN

Origen's greatest work on Scripture was **The Hexapla**. This monumental volume contained five different texts of the Old

Testament in six parallel columns which enabled scholars to make critical comparisons of the texts very quickly. He also wrote other biblical works: short explanations of difficult passages, commentaries on texts for the purpose of instructing the faithful, homilies. One of the methods he used to explain Scripture was the allegorical or symbolic style. This technique was innovative in his day and caused him some problems because it tended to move away from the literal sense of the Scriptures. On the other hand, it opened up a more prayerful approach and later won him the reputation of being one of the Church's mystical theologians.

In theology, **De Principiis** (the principal articles of the teachings of the Church) was written when he was a mature man of forty. **Contra Celsum** ("against Celsus"), an apologetic work, was written in the style of a dialogue which makes it interesting reading. In **Exhortation to Martyrdom**, Origen encouraged two friends about to be martyred not to give way to fear when suffering for Christ. He exhorted them, instead, to jump for joy since they had been found worthy to suffer like the Apostles.

But the writing which perhaps appeals most to moderns is **On Prayer**. It is the most ancient work we have today explaining prayer in a systematized way. The naming of the traditional types of prayer which we are familiar with (adoration, petition, thanksgiving, contrition) is attributed to Origen. **On Prayer** gives testimony to the inner depth of the man. It was his belief that we should not ask for small things because God wants to give us great things. He also reminds us that we do not pray to influence God but, rather, to share in his life.

CONCLUSION

Origen lived in unsettled and turbulent times. As a result, history has not always been kind to him. Some of his teachings were considered erroneous but, despite this fact, he himself was never formally declared a heretic. He was not only a genius but a very holy man. The historian Eusebius did not hesitate to call him the "supreme saint." Despite his great intelligence he did not consider perfection to consist in knowledge as did St. Clement of Alexandria, but rather in works of charity. And though he was never canonically declared a saint by the Church, he is without doubt one of the greatest among the Fathers of the Church.

In his writing **On Prayer** we discover a humble man through his own words:

> **...If we know not God and know not the things of God, neither will we know of what we are in need.**

> **...All our life must be a prayer without ceasing in which we say: OUR FATHER WHO ART IN HEAVEN.**

> **...It is enjoined that everyone, in order to pray in peace and without disturbance, should choose a special place in their own house, if there is room for it—our sanctuary, so to speak—and there we should pray.**

CYPRIAN

Discerner of Spirits

Few of us have such ardent admirers that they are willing to stretch the truth of our lives a bit to make us look good. St. Cyprian did. In fact, the only biography we have of him, written by his deacon, Pontius, is a classic demonstration of extravagant hero-worship. For this reason, unfortunately, it is historically unreliable. Those who have tried to search out the facts of Cyprian's life say he was born sometime between 200-210 A.D. in Africa, probably in Carthage, where he was educated as a pagan in a wealthy and cultivated society.

St. Jerome tells us he began his professional life as a rhetorician. Others say he worked, rather, in government, surmised from the easy familiarity with constitutional laws and political ideas evidenced in his writings (later transferred into the administration of his diocese). Whichever secular career he pursued, Cyprian was not long in either. He became a Christian under the priest Caecilius, giving his fortune to the poor and, shortly afterward, was ordained. His first writing, dealing with his conversion, describes what he called "pagan abominations": wars, gladiatorial fights, the theater, the excesses of immorality and corruption which he witnessed in public and private life. His election as bishop of Carthage in 248 or 249 originated through the will of the people against the opposition of some elderly presbyters. One writer described him as a born leader, not only of lay people, but of bishops; some even called him the "Pope of Africa."

Today, spiritual directors concerned with discerning spirits might well look to Cyprian as a model. He was severely tested in this process during the persecution of Decian (c. 250 A.D.). Pope Fabian was martyred in the persecution while Cyprian, choosing to go into hiding, was spared. Even though the beliefs of Tertullian and the Montanists concerning the obligation of martyrdom were not so strongly in force during this period, the priests and deacons of Rome severely criticized him for this "escape." From hindsight, however, we can see that Cyprian felt that living for his people was more important than dying for them at that particular time. He prefaced a letter to his detractors with, "What I have done and am doing has been told to you in a somewhat garbled and untruthful manner." He indicated this exile was only a temporary stance and presented some of the motivation which preceded his decision: to pacify brethren who insisted to the point of violence that he hide; to counsel his people from afar; to strengthen and console those being persecuted; to maintain ecclesiastical discipline in the Church.

Prior to this voluntary exile his property was confiscated. A large body of works, written during his exile, give us a good picture of the Church around the middle of the third century. The most reliable information we have about Cyprian's life concerns his arrest, trial and martyrdom. These are found in the official reports, **Acta Proconsularia Cypriani**. During the persecution of Valerian, Cyprian, more sure of the faith of his congregation this time, could afford them the example of martyrdom. The account tells us he was banished to Curubix where, after he had been taken into custody, a large crowd, wishing to die with him, followed him. The sentence was carried out after a formal interrogation the next day.

The saint took off his robe, knelt for a last prayer and then waited for the end, asking those in charge to pay the executioner some gold pieces for the trouble of carrying out his task. With this, he was blindfolded and the people spread linen cloths to catch his blood. He was beheaded September 14, 258 A.D., the first African bishop to be martyred. His body, buried immediately at the site of execution to "remove it from the curiosity of the pagans," was reclaimed later that same night and carried by Christians who held torches and candles and who prayed loudly in jubilation; then they buried him with solemnity elsewhere.

St. Cyprian's personality can be discovered chiefly in his literary works which were directly tied to his life and time. All were written for specific occasions and served the very practical purpose of directing his people. Because of his pastoral bent they are not too concerned with theological speculation. His language and style are clear and he was greatly influenced by the vocabulary and imagery of the Bible. For this reason, though his works are less insightful than Tertullian's, more of them have been preserved through the years because they were popular during the Middle Ages. He was the most widely read Father of the Church at the time and considered *the* theological authority of the West up to the time of Augustine.

Most scholars agree that he depended heavily on Tertullian for his ideas. St. Jerome claims that Cyprian read Tertullian's works every day, asking his secretary frequently to "hand me the master." However, the two men were opposite in personality. While Tertullian was superior in profundity and originality as a thinker, Cyprian seems to have been more charitable, gentle and prudent. Some writers object to such comparisons of the two, asserting that their upbringing was distinctly different, as well as the times in which they lived. These scholars point out that Cyprian was born into the higher circles of society while Tertullian was a soldier's child.

Because of his more comfortable circumstances, Cyprian owned lands, had a good and thorough education and was self-assured in social circles; he also had advantageous connections with authorities. Moreover, though he, like Tertullian, lived in turbulent political times, the Church itself was more established. Its organizational structure was more consolidated and it had a distinct tradition uniting the bishops with their congregations. Perhaps, rather than compare, it would be better to rejoice that the unique characteristics of each of them have added to the diversity we find in the Church; both sugar and spice are needed to give it a fuller, richer life.

CYPRIAN AS PASTOR

The scope of Cyprian's writings gives us an idea of his pastoral orientation. Consider these topics: Christology, Church unity, Scripture, Baptism, Eucharist, Penance, prayer, the power of grace (to encourage others to follow his own example of conversion), authority, apologetics, morality and ecclesiastical discipline, morality and martyrdom (for those under persecution), works and almsgiving to relieve the poor (he himself once aided the plague-stricken), patience (following Tertullian's lead here), jealousy, envy and even a letter on the dress of virgins! Three books, a compendium of scriptural passages, are important to us as a history of the oldest Latin versions of the Bible.

Cyprian's influence on the development of canon law was very strong. One of the problems he had to deal with during his exile led to his teachings on excommunication and reconciliation, some of which are still in force today. During the persecution some Christians compromised their faith out of fear and offered sacrifice to the Emperor's gods. This done, they, aided by some priests in Cyprian's absence, wished immediate reconciliation with the Church. One of his most important works, **De Lapsis**, deals with the problem by designating the time of penance needed before reconciliation. If in danger of death, however, no one was to be refused absolution. Our system of classification of sins according to their gravity stems from this period.

Eventually, the priests involved in the question broke with the Church. This schism led Cyprian to write his most famous work, **The Unity of the Church**, in which he asserted that heresies and schisms were the work of the devil. The much quoted statement "outside the Church there is no salvation" is found in this writing. In it, he declared that we could not have God for our Father unless the Church were our Mother. He called the Church the seamless robe of Christ and compares it to many things: the ark of Noah, many grains—one bread, a ship with the bishop as a pilot, the Mother who has the whole family in her bosom and so on.

He agreed with Tertullian that Baptism conferred by heretics was invalid, but he disagreed with his master on the subject of infant Baptism. He wanted Baptism conferred as early as possible, even suggesting within two or three days of birth. His dominant idea on the Eucharist was that it was a sacrifice, a re-presentation of Christ's sacrifice on the cross; he declared also that the bread and wine were the bond of ecclesiastical unity as well as the bond between Christ and the faithful.

His writings on authority are ambiguous. At one point he stated, "Whoever is not with the bishop is not in the Church." At other times he emphasized the community of bishops, that is, the episcopal college. Perhaps he is the patron of collegiality as well as of discernment. As far as the primacy of the bishop of Rome was concerned, Cyprian seems to have held the theory, stemming from the time of Ignatius of Antioch, of an episcopate without a papacy, all the bishops being equal. However, as some historians point out, he was not always consistent in this view, for he did seem to recognize his own obligation to report occasionally to Rome on matters of importance. It may be that he saw the bishop of Rome having a primacy of honor rather than of jurisdiction.

God seems to have played a practical trick on Cyprian in this regard at the end of his life. Much of his time was spent in dealing with the controversy of the baptisms conferred by heretics. Three synods and a council of the African bishops, presided over by Cyprian, declared these baptisms invalid. Cyprian, holding to his view that all bishops are equal, cast his vote last about the matter in order to underscore this point. Pope Stephen (254-256) sharply rebuked them for this decision, but Cyprian did not revoke it. Just when the dispute was threatening to become serious, the edict of Valerian against Christians brought Carthage and Rome together by necessity and both men died for the same faith.

In a treatise on the "Our Father," we see that Cyprian's pastoral efforts extended also to the prayer life of his people. He believed this prayer contained the whole Christian faith; from his treatise we get an insight into his own relationship to Christ:

It is a loving and friendly prayer to beseech God with his own Word, to come up to his ears in the prayer of Christ. Let the Father acknowledge the words of his Son when we

make our prayer, and let the One who dwells within our breast also dwell in our voice... For since he says, that "whatsoever we shall ask of the Father in his name, he will give us," how much more effectually do we obtain what we ask in Christ's name, if we ask for it in his own prayer. (Treatise IV, #3).

METHODIUS

In Praise of the Little Ones

Methodius, one of the minor Fathers of the Church, is so classified because very little is known about him and because so few
of his writings contributed significantly to the development of
Church doctrine. Some of his writings were lost and some attributed to him are of doubtful authorship. As a result, he did not
emerge as one of the great Fathers. Nevertheless, a few works
did survive and the praise Methodius received from many
ancient writers compensates in part for some of the obscurity
which, due to unfortunate historical circumstances, shrouds his
life and works. One scholar at least made the wry suggestion that
Eusebius, irked by Methodius' dislike for Origen's ideas, did not
mention him in his **Ecclesiastical History**.

One writer reports that Methodius was born around 260 A.D.;
most historians agree that he suffered martyrdom around 311-
312 A.D., though there is a difference of opinion as to whether
he suffered under Decius and Valerian or Diocletian. Some say
he was the bishop of Olympus; others say he was bishop of both
Olympus and Patara in Lycia (Asia Minor). One author states he
was probably bishop of Philippi in Macedonia also, while another claims it is not certain whether he was a bishop at all.

Doctrinally a traditional thinker, Methodius was not as creative as his opponent Origen. He did have a creative bent, however, for he used the ideas and methods of other persons as if
they were his own, arriving at different conclusions. For example, he took the title, "second Eve," as applied to Mary by St.
Irenaeus and extended it to refer to the Church. In his works he

used the method of dialogue found in the classics, especially Plato, whom he read avidly. Strangely, the allegories he employs in his greatest work, "The Banquet of the Ten Virgins," give evidence of his having been influenced by Origen.

In this work, Methodius sees virginity as the perfect Christian life, a pre-eminent way of imitating Christ. In one passage from the work, he discusses virginity from a point of view which is interesting in the light of modern psychology. He describes it as a gradual historical process. Humankind, according to this thought, was not ready at first for such an exalted state as virginity; it moved in the course of time from the "childhood" of intermarriage within families to polygamy, to monogamy, to continence within marriage until it finally arrived at the mature "adulthood" of virginity.

Though Methodius extolled virginity in a way we moderns might find disconcerting—calling it at various times the "brightest and most glorious star of Christ," "perfection," "a means of reconciliation to God," "pure, unalloyed gold," "a spring flower exhaling immortality," "a lily and a martyrdom," and so on, he does recognize marriage as an acceptable life-style. In one instance he compares the two in this way: "...although the moon may be greater than the stars, the light of the other stars is not destroyed by the moonlight."

One of the most interesting sections of "The Banquet of the Ten Virgins" is that in which Methodius shows how truly Christ was one of us. He used Jeremiah's story of the potter, whose pottery, upon completion, was marred. The potter re-made his work of art into a new creation out of the same clay. He goes on to explain that Christ, similarly, is a kind of "re-worked" Adam:

For when Adam, having been formed out of clay, was still soft and moist, and not yet like a tile made hard and incorruptible, sin ruined him, flowing and dropping down upon him like water. And therefore God, moistening him afresh and forming anew the same clay to his honor, having first hardened and fixed it in the Virgin's womb, and united and mixed it with the Word, brought

**it forth into life no longer soft and broken; lest, being
overflowed again by streams of corruption from without,
it should become soft and perish (TBTV, 4).**

Indeed, Scripture alludes to this truth itself when speaking of
Christ as the second Adam (see Rom. 5:12-20).

His treatise "Concerning Free Will" is an argument against
the dualistic beliefs of the Gnostics. It, too, is in dialogue form;
in it he tells a friend about a reverie he had one day while walking along the seashore. He observed the sea and all the other
creatures of the earth and was fascinated by the orderly arrangement which existed everywhere in the universe. When he came
upon two men, however, he discovered them fighting with one
another and stripping a third person. The orderly arrangement
which he had observed before was now suddenly disturbed. From
the vantage point of this story, Methodius goes on to explain that
evil is neither eternal, nor material, nor does it originate in God,
but is solely the result of our free will: "...man after his creation
receives a commandment from God; and from this at once rises
evil, for he does not obey the divine command; and this alone is
evil, namely, disobedience, which had a beginning."

In his "Discourse on the Resurrection," the concrete imagery
which Methodius uses to describe Christ is carried over and
applied to us. He did not, as Origen, see the body as a fetter or
hindrance to the soul; he criticized him also for over-spiritualiz-
ing the resurrected body, reasoning this way: "Christ truly was
made man, and died, not in mere appearance, but that he might
truly be shown to be the first begotten from the dead, changing
the earthy into the heavenly, and the mortal into the immortal"
(DR 1, 113). He declares that our own bodies will rise, transformed, it is true, but nevertheless, real bodies.

Death, according to Methodius, is a necessary process, "...in
order that, by the dissolution of the body, sin might be altogether destroyed from the very roots, that there might not be left
even the smallest particle of root from which new shoots of sin
might again burst forth" (DR 1, 4). In another passage, insisting
that humans will not be like angels in heaven, without bodies, he

argues that God, who does not do things without purpose, created this diversity among beings and does not intend to wipe it out in heaven:

> **For Christ at his coming did not proclaim that the human nature should, when it is immortal, be remolded or transformed into another nature, but into what it was before the fall. For each one among created things must remain in its own proper place, that none may be wanting to any, but all may be full: heaven of angels; thrones of powers; luminaries of ministers; and the more divine spots and the undefiled and untainted luminaries, with seraphim, who attend the Supreme Council, and uphold the universe; and the world of humans (DR 1, 10-emphasis editor's).**

Consistent with his "earthy" teaching to the end, Methodius affirms, further, that heaven is a concrete place. Indeed, it is this world transformed "...from its present condition to a better and more glorious one..." With a touch of impatience, he ends this passage with, "Wherefore it is silly to discuss in what way of life our bodies will then exist, if there is no longer air, nor earth, nor anything else" (DR 1, 9).

ANTHONY
THE GREAT

Master of Simple Living

Most of us are familiar with the well-loved St. Anthony of Padua, if for no other reason than his reputation for finding lost objects. Less celebrated, perhaps, is St. Anthony known as "the Hermit" or "of the Desert," despite his additional title, "the Great," received because of the character of his life and because he founded the first monasteries in the history of the Church. Most of the information we have about him is found in St. Athanasius' biography, **Life of Anthony**.

Though written within a year of Anthony's death, this account does not measure up to the usual standards demanded by historians, for it was written for the edification of the monks who followed the saint. It therefore tends to be somewhat subjective and moralizing in tone. But what the work lacks in strictly factual data is compensated for in its reputation, for some scholars claim that this document contributed more than any other factor in the spread of monastic life.

According to Athanasius, Anthony was born in Egypt around 250 A.D. of well-to-do Christian parents. He was very attached to his home life, preferring it to life in school or the companionship of other children. When his parents died he became the owner of a huge estate. One day, however, on entering a church, he heard the words, "If you will be perfect, go sell all that you have and give to the poor..." (Mt. 19:21). As happens with us sometimes, he felt these words were directed to himself.

Consequently, he gave away all his lands to the poor and sold most of his estate, giving this money to the poor as well, reserving only what was absolutely necessary to maintain himself and his sister. Soon after, however, the incident repeated itself similarly, and with the words, "Be not solicitous for the morrow" (Mt. 6:34) ringing in his ears, he relinquished the fund reserved for his sister, putting her in the care of a group of virgins. This is the first recorded hint we have in history of what we might call "nuns" today. With this final act of deprivation, Anthony began the practice of a strict ascetic life near his old home.

His life combined prayer with fasting and manual labor, the latter in order to earn his living. The lives of the other ascetics he knew became the training ground for his own practices:

He observed the graciousness of one, the earnestness at prayer in another; studied the even temper of one and the kindheartedness of another; fixed his attention on the vigils kept by one and on the studies pursued by another; admired one for his patient endurance, another for his fasting and sleeping on the ground; watched closely this person's meekness and the forbearance shown by another; and in one and all alike he marked especially devotion to Christ and the love they had for one another (LOA, p. 21).

It is interesting to note, for the benefit of students and their parents, that "study" was one of the virtues esteemed by Anthony.

Two themes predominate throughout the **Life of Anthony**: the temptations and ascetical feats accomplished by the saintly hermit. Temptations came in suggestions to abandon his purpose, to return and take care of his sister, to seek fame, food and pleasures, especially those of the flesh. The response Anthony gave to all these temptations reads as follows in the **Life**. Its starkness should resonate with moderns searching for a simple life.

**ANTHONY
THE GREAT**

> **...he ate but once a day, after sunset; indeed, sometimes only every other day, and frequently only every fourth day did he partake of food. His food was bread and salt; his drink, water only. Meat and wine we need not even mention, for no such thing could be found with the other ascetics either. He was content to sleep on a rush mat, though as a rule he lay down on the bare ground (p. 25).**

After he felt he had mastered these temptations sufficiently, he moved to the outskirts of the village, setting up residence in tombs. The temptations he endured there were of a type and intensity that can chill our bones as much as any horror films on diabolical possession. He was lashed by demons, had phantoms and even experienced a shaking of his dwelling. Finally ready for further combat, Anthony left for the desert seeking even greater solitude. Along the way he was tempted by the illusions of silver and gold scattered along the road, but he persevered and eventually walled himself up in a deserted fort on the side of a mountain, referred to as the "Outer Mountain," near the Nile, where he experienced ecstasies as well as even greater temptations.

To encourage other monks in their own asceticism, Anthony claimed, "Often visions are granted as a compensation for its hardships." So dearly did he treasure his solitude that he would not allow anyone, even his friends, to come into his hermitage. Far from resenting this, his admirers came and spent whole nights out in the cold desert near his hermitage just to be near this holy person. Many, persuaded by Anthony that this was a desirable way of life, followed his example, and it was not long before the desert became populated with monks. It was evident he was a leader despite his solitariness. After establishing others in his way of life, he retreated further into the desert region, settling at the foothills of what his biographer calls the "Inner Mountain."

Though an avowed hermit, loving his solitude—"Just as fish exposed for any length of time on dry land die, so monks go to pieces when they loiter among you and spend too much time with you. Therefore, we must be off to the mountain as fish to the sea" (p. 90)—he was not a selfish solitary. The few times he left his hermitage were for the purpose of assisting other Christians and the Church in general. During the persecution of Maximim, he went to the prisons and courtrooms encouraging those about to suffer martyrdom. Once he went to Alexandria to denounce the Arians. His saintly life and wise counsels also reached out to touch emperors—including Constantine and his sons, who wrote to the holy man seeking his advice. And one time, at the request of some monks, he left his solitude to visit the monastic settlements along the Nile which had originated at his inspiration. On this particular visit we are happy to note he paid a visit to his sister. The account tells us he "...rejoiced to witness the zeal of the monks and his sister grown old in her virginity, herself the guiding spirit of other virgins" (p. 66).

The biography includes more than Anthony's extraordinary asceticisms, his conquering of temptations, the guidance he rendered others and the example he gave solely by his presence in the desert. There are also accounts of wonders performed: cures from disease and paralysis, the expelling of demons, gifts of prophecy. Of the latter, one was his foretelling of the atrocities committed by the Arians against the Church in the middle of the fourth century. To the saint, however, these gifts were of little account. As Athanasius records, "As for Anthony, this alone was wonderful, that as he sat with sober heart on the mountain, the Lord showed him things afar off" (p. 70).

In regard to prayer, Anthony was a source of strength to others who might otherwise be discouraged when it seemed their prayer had not been answered, for "he neither boasted when he was heard, not did he complain when not heard" (p. 68). Athanasius tells us he habitually found solutions for his problems through prayer and that he was, as Scripture describes, a man truly "taught of God." The hermit frequently used the Sign of the Cross as a way of dispelling temptation, saying, "Where the Sign of the Cross appears, there magic is powerless and sorcery ineffectual" (p. 84). A further indication of the vibrant interior life of this man can be found in another section where Anthony declared that the demonic one, "hearing the Savior's name, was unable to endure the heat it caused in him" (p. 55), and, again, a rather amusing passage tells us the demon went up in smoke at Anthony's rebuke!

Some parts of the **Life** might lead us to wonder if the saint were not somewhat "anti-intellectual," but Athanasius insists that "his speech was seasoned with a divine wisdom" despite his lack of schooling and his lack of desire to have such. In a very long section of the biography we find Anthony lecturing the pagans, in rebuttal to their rational arguments, with these words: "...it is not wordcraft which we have, but faith through love that works for Christ" (p. 86). Anthony felt Sacred Scripture was sufficient for our instruction.

When Anthony received a premonition of his death, he was concerned that those who loved him might follow the custom of the Egyptians of preserving his body in their homes. To prevent this, he stayed in the Inner Mountain where only two ascetics attended him in his old age. These he swore to secrecy regarding his burial place, and so the secret remains to our own day.

Among the important legacies he left us, other than his life, were his teachings, two of which seem remarkably contemporary. One of these might be called "suggestions for discernment of spirits." Not only did Anthony encourage others to pray and practice ascetic discipline "for the gift of discerning spirits" and "not put faith in every spirit" (p. 52), but he suggested also that "every man daily take an accounting with himself of the day's and the night's doings" (p. 67). One wonders if Anthony were the originator of the "prayer journal" when he suggests, "...let us each note and write down our actions and impulses of the soul as though we were to report them to each other; and you may rest assured that from utter shame of becoming known we shall stop sinning and entertaining sinful thoughts altogether. ...let the written account stand for the eyes of our fellow ascetics, so that blushing at writing the same as if we were actually seen, we may never ponder evil" (p. 68).

Finally, the second teaching having a familiar, incarnational ring deals with the practice of a virtuous life. Far from trying to urge others on to a "supernatural" state, he believed that "virtue exists when the soul keeps in its natural state. It is kept in its natural state when it remains as it came into being" (p. 37). Anthony wants us to return to our original condition, which Christ, the new Adam, has made possible for us to regain. So to "do what comes naturally," for Anthony, is virtue and to pervert nature, vice. He pleads, "...having received the soul as something entrusted to us, let us guard it for the Lord, that he may recognize his work as being the same as he made it" (p. 38).

PACHOMIUS

A Hermit Turned
Communitarian

Years ago, participating in a Better World Movement retreat, I was jolted by the opening statement of our director: "Jesus said, 'By this will all men know that you are my disciples, if you have love one for another.' I would suggest that, after hundreds of years of Christianity, this is the only proof not tried by Christians so far." I can still feel the puzzlement and consternation the statement evoked in us. It had in it echoes of G.K. Chesterton's sobering comment that Christianity had not been tried and found wanting; it simply had not been tried.

Though we may have to admit to the truth of the retreat director's words in our own time, apparently the rebuke cannot be laid at the feet of Christians in every century. Pachomius of Egypt, at least, is striking proof that the opposite was true. Born of pagan parents in Thebaid around 292 A.D., he was captured at age twenty and made a recruit for Constantine's army. While he was in prison, of all places, his conversion was occasioned by Christians who, bringing food and drink to the incarcerated, impressed him as being "merciful to everyone even strangers" (**Life of Pachomius, #4, p. 7**).

The most authentic information we have on this originator of Christian cenobitic (community) living is found in the **Life of Pachomius** and the **Rule of Pachomius**. The **Life** as we have it today comes from various sources—Coptic, Arabic, Syriac, Greek. Scholars claim this because of the different emphases given to

74

certain aspects of Pachomius' life. Though some hold the Coptic as basis for all other versions, many favor the Greek as being the best. Of the half dozen biographies, some may have been written no more than fifteen or twenty years after the death of Pachomius. By 404 A.D. his monasteries could be found as far away as the northeastern part of Alexandria. As a result, St. Jerome was asked to translate the **Rule** into Latin to make it available in other regions. It was this translation which allowed Pachomius' work to have influence on the rules of the West, particularly the **Rule of St. Benedict.** The **Life** follows the style of most biographies of the time; it has an underlying historical basis accompanied by some embellishments inserted by devoted followers of the hero of the story.

Keeping this in mind, we are told that on the night of his baptism, Pachomius had a vision of dew (symbolizing Baptism) from heaven falling on him. As the dew gathered in his right hand, it turned into solid honey (symbolizing Eucharist) which fell upon the earth. At the same time, he heard someone say, "Heed what is taking place, for it shall come to pass in the future" (LP, #5, p. 9). After this, he went to an old hermit nearby and asked to become a monk. Palamon tried to dissuade him, saying the life was extremely hard. But for Pachomius, renunciation was so essential to monastic life (his definition of a monk was simply, "one who renounces") that, instead, he ended up persuading the anchorite of his earnest intentions, and followed his way of life in all its rigor until the latter's death. This period of Pachomius' life, together with the interim period preceding his baptism, constituted his novitiate which formed his unique expression of monastic life in the years to come.

According to Palladius in the **Lausiac History,** the **Rule of Pachomius** was dictated to him by an angel. At the same time the angel was supposed to have instructed him about his future life-style:

To him as he sat in his cave an angel appeared and said: "You have successfully ordered your own life. So it is superfluous to remain sitting in your cave. Up! Go out

**and collect all the young monks and dwell with them,
and according to the model which I now give you, so leg-
islate for them"; and he gave him a brass tablet...**

In the **Life of Pachomius**, a similar heavenly visitation took
place. An angel said, "Stay here and build a monastery, and many
will come to you to become monks" (LP, #12, p. 17). Elsewhere in
the **Life** a comment is made that after Pachomius "thought about
the voice which he heard and realized its meaning, he started
receiving those who came to him" (LP, #24, p. 29).

Because of discrepancies in various works and through scientific study of texts, most scholars would, without denying the
possibility of visions, admit these probably did not take place. It
is more likely that Pachomius, like every monastic founder,
groped and searched until he found the best way to express what
he felt God was calling him to do. The end result we call the
"vision" or "charism" of the founder, or, if written down, the
"rule" of the founder. As some authors point out, Pachomius
had relatively few visions and when he did they always are
described as taking place at prayer. It is probably realistic to say
he struggled from day to day to know the will of God and, as it
is with all of us, the closer he came to his own heart, the inner
core of his own being, the greater became the possibility for
realizing what God wanted him to do. History has proven that
he did discover a true internal call during prayer: his basic life-
style endures even today.

How did Pachomius develop his vision of community living?
First of all, from the Christians who had been good to him in
prison; their deeds became the seed for the manner of life he
eventually organized. As a result, he promised God he would
serve him and seek his whole will all his life. After his brief stay
in the army and in prison, he settled in Upper Thebaid where
he became a catechumen. During the interim period before his
baptism he grew vegetables, helping those who came to him in
whatever way he could. Soon groups of people formed around
him because he was good to them.

Many who came were pagans, so entering the monastery for

them meant entering the Church. In a short span of twenty-two years (from around 324 when his first disciples came until his death in 346) his life-style took firm root. It is interesting to note also that he established the first community of monastic women. With his own sister heading the group, they followed the **Rule** of the monks. Basically, Pachomius saw the life of the apostles as the model for community living. The apostles lived constantly with Jesus, left everything to follow him and were with him in his trials. We see here the principles of monastic living: living together (community) in union with Jesus (prayer), renouncing all for him (asceticism).

Pachomius' new life-style incorporated modified ideas from his eremitical days. Tensions resulted, not the least of which was his desire both for solitude and for community. His approach to these tensions gives us insights into his personality. For example, he said the Gospel presents the ideal so that monks could attain at least to some of the renunciation required by "hating" one's father and mother in order to follow Jesus. In this instance, we see the tension of his desire for a profound detachment from all things versus a very human desire to respect one's family. Worked out in practice, Pachomius allowed his monks to visit sick relatives providing they did not neglect any religious duties. If a relative gave a monk food, he was not to keep it; instead, he was to give it to the porter (a kind of monastic receptionist) who would, in turn, give it to the infirmary, reserving a small portion of it for the monk!

Other regulations had equally humorous results; nevertheless, the motivation behind Pachomius' renunciations was peculiarly Christian: family and things were renounced to enable monks to commit themselves to Someone, to imitate Christ who was obedient to death, to attain purity of heart, to do penance for their sins, to remain alert to the attacks of the devil and to come to self-knowledge. The renunciations involved in a life of poverty witnessed their trust in the providence of God and their solidarity with the poor and suffering everywhere.

A tension arose also between stability and mobility. Pachomius wanted his monks to practice stability, but, finding that local superiors tended to become attached to their monasteries, he changed them from one place to another frequently. This tendency toward attachment filtered into every area it seems. Pachomius did not want his monks to become priests because it might be a source of pride, as was the holding of important offices in the community. Some became attached to comfort or even to their abilities to fast.

Though the **Rule** gives detailed instructions on such things as eating, drinking, work, sleep, clothing and so on, Pachomius founded a very balanced life-style. He neither expected his monks to do anything he himself was unwilling to do nor did he oblige anyone to do anything unless he understood what was being asked of him. If he demanded personal asceticism he was equally strong in requiring the monastery to provide for the needs of the monks. While legislating for chastity, manual labor, vigils, endurance in illness, fasting, silence, simplicity in housing and clothing as bodily asceticisms, he stressed that none of these had any worth unless backed up by humility, obedience and more important values.

Pachomius did not have an elaborate system of prayer, but from the **Rule** we learn how the community prayed and, therefore, how they viewed prayer. Like the desert monks they tried to pray unceasingly. They prayed while they worked. Periodically, a monk would go to a kind of podium and recite a prayer or some Scripture by heart. Then those working would rise, recite the Our Father and prostrate themselves for a moment before going back to their weaving or other work. They gathered together for more formal prayer at the beginning and end of each day when they simply prayed aloud what they had been praying personally all day long. Pachomius insisted that his monks learn to read, not to become intellectuals, but for the purpose of reading Scripture, vast sections of which they would then commit to memory. When someone new came to the monastery, his introduction to the community was his being given a place in the assembly of prayer—clearly indicating its primacy in their life. The Eucharist, about which there is little legislation, was celebrated twice a week at the local church.

Physical healing and visions were regarded as having little importance to this monastic leader. He loved others, not by saying, "I love you," but by challenging them to leave sinful lives and to turn to the Lord; thus, conversion and reconciliation were, for him, the greatest services of healing. When requested to tell about his visions, he asked, "What is a greater vision than to see the invisible God in the visible person who is his temple?" (LP, #48, p. 69). We moderns can hardly quarrel with that kind of theology!

MACRINA

Woman of Influence

The **Life of Macrina,** written by her younger and famous brother, Gregory of Nyssa, is one of the earliest biographies of a
woman available to us today. The official view of women in her
day was that no matter how holy, they could not qualify as
"teachers of the Church." She was the eldest of ten children in a
wealthy, long-established Cappadocian family which had been
tried and tested during the persecutions of Diocletian. Her
grandparents were forced to flee for safety to the mountains of
Pontus and her maternal grandfather even lost his life and all
his possessions for his opposition to the emperor. Further
emphasizing that Macrina came from "holy seed," Gregory
praises the life of their mother, Emmelia, who, if she could have
had her way, would have remained unmarried. However, when
she risked abuse from the ardent suitors who sought her for her
beauty, she decided to choose one of them, Basil, well-known
for his virtue, as her husband.

While still pregnant with Macrina, she had a dream in which
she was carrying her unborn child in her hands. According to
the account, a magnificent being appeared and addressed the
child three times as "Thecla"—after a famous legendary virgin.
From then on, this was her secret name though her family insisted she be called "Macrina" after her saintly paternal grandmother who "in the time of the persecutions had contended as a
confessor on behalf of Christ" (**Life of Macrina**). The result was
that the secret name was meant chiefly to foretell the kind of
life the child would lead. Though we do not know the exact

dates of Macrina's life, some speculate that she was born in 327 A.D., which would situate her in the early fourth century around the time of the Council of Nicaea. Further clues of the time in which she lived come from knowing Gregory was her brother and that Gregory of Nazianus and Evagrius were friends of her younger brother Basil.

As was the custom, Macrina had her own nurse as a child, but, nevertheless, her primary teacher was her mother who determined that her education would not be that of the secular society in which she lived. She believed it was shameful to teach children "either the sentiments of tragedy which concern women or the indecencies of comedy, or the reasons for Troy's evils," all of which would defile the child with unseemly stories about women (**Women in the Early Church** by Elizabeth A. Clark, Michael Glazier, Inc., Wilmington, DE, 1983, p. 238). Instead she fed her with Sacred Scripture which became the foundation of her study, especially the Wisdom of Solomon. In fact, she led a kind of religious life in her younger years, chanting the Psalms in between work, meals and rest. As Gregory puts it, "...always she had the Psalms with her like a good travelling companion who never fails" (LM). The craft that she practiced was wool-working.

Gregory, in the **Life**, extravagantly extols Macrina's beauty, saying no artist could possibly reproduce or encompass it. Her father, he claims, deluged by potential suitors for her hand, decided to betroth her to the most promising of them when she came of age. Meanwhile, the young man he had in mind suddenly died. Macrina persuaded her father that his decision had constituted, in fact, an actual marriage. She reasoned convincingly that since marriage, like birth and death, was unique and her young man still lived in God, it would be unnatural for her to marry someone else. To secure this desire to remain unmarried, she attached herself devotedly to the care of her mother from then on, never leaving her presence. She cooked, baked bread, and co-administered her mother's extensive properties in the provinces. They nourished each other physically and spiritually, and, primarily at Macrina's instigation, spurred each other on by the simple life-style they lived.

The **Life of Macrina** was written sometime between 380-383 A.D. It was written at the request of a fellow ecclesiastic who wanted more information about her. He apologized for stretching "the limits of a letter" and gave as his reason "that the subject on which you directed me to write is greater than is commensurate to a letter" (ibid.). He expressed some reluctance to call her "'a woman' for I do not know if it is appropriate to call her by a name taken from nature when she surpassed that nature"—a comment which not only expressed his esteem for Macrina but indicated the general attitude toward women in his day.

It is clear Macrina was overshadowed by her famous family; yet her life was glorified by Gregory. The reason? One author suggests she outshone them all. When she was twelve she helped bring up the family after the death of her saintly father, thus exerting great influence over them. For the youngest, Peter, she was, in Gregory's words, "father, guide, mother." Sometime after her sisters had left home to start their own families, her brother Basil returned from school where he had been trained in rhetoric. Macrina found him somewhat obnoxious in his pride over his newly-acquired abilities (Gregory says, "monstrously conceited"). She intuitively led him so skillfully toward the goal of philosophy that he soon expressed contempt at being an "object of marvel" on account of his rhetoric. Then he began to live a simple life of manual labor and poverty.

At the same time, she guided her mother, St. Emmelia, to give up the service she had been receiving from her maids and to live a less ostentatious life. In short, around 340 Macrina had transformed their home into a monastery where possessions were held in common and the servants were treated as sisters and brothers. Later she persuaded her brother Basil to found a monastery. Still later she persuaded her brother Gregory to join him in a life of prayer and study until Basil, by that time the great Patriarch of the East, insisted he take up the duties of bishop of Nyssa.

An interesting aside resulting from Gregory's role as bishop gives us an insight into the personalities of the brother and sister. Due to his ignorance of worldly affairs, he was charged with embezzlement by the Arian ruler Valens who banished him to

Selucia. In a touching passage from the **Life** he confides his circumstances to Macrina who replies:

> **Will you not put an end to your failure to recognize the good things which come from God? ... Churches send you forth and call upon you as ally and reformer, and you do not see the grace in this? Do you not even realize the true cause of such great blessings, that your parents' prayers are lifting you on high, for you have little or no native capacity for this?**

We see Gregory as a gentle, humble man who trusts his older sister and does not mind admitting, with candor and humor, her rebuke. Nor does he deny that it was a just reproach. It is not an exaggeration to say that Macrina was a major founder of the Cappadocian ascetic life and ultimately, because of her influence on Basil, of Basilian monasticism. Can we perhaps call her a "desert mother" insofar as she lived a life "hidden" both within her family and within the commonly held view toward women in her day?

A description of the family under Macrina's influence is spelled out by Gregory in rather idealistic terms:

> **... In them no anger, envy, hate, arrogance, nor any other such thing was seen; the desire for foolish things of no substance, for honor, glory, delusions of grandeur, the need to be superior to others, and all such things had been eradicated. Self-control was their pleasure, not to be known was their fame; their wealth was in possessing nothing and in shaking off all material surplus like dust from the body; their work was none of the concerns of this life, except insofar as it was a subordinate task. Their only care was for divine realities, and there was constant prayer and the unceasing singing of hymns, extended equally throughout the entire day and night so that this was both work and respite for them... (ibid.).**

Macrina's great beauty is not the only attribute Gregory extols. In his account of her death, he compares her to the intellectual stature of the great Socrates. Indeed, he presents her as the Christian Socrates, equal to or even surpassing that giant in the world of philosophy. Since her early training was primarily Sacred Scripture, some historians argue about just how much expertise she had in that field. They suggest that it belongs, rather, to Gregory who wants to place her under his own mantle of knowledge. Others, on the other hand, point out that just as some uneducated but intelligent people become self-educated, so Macrina, the primary teacher and guide in a family made up of philosophers, theologians and bishops, could easily have acquired philosophical learning. This possibility is strengthened when we discover that she often debated with Gregory regarding theological and philosophical questions. Hers was the most intellectual family of the fourth century.

Gregory describes his sister's last hours in detail. When he arrived at the convent he found her lying on a bare floor. On seeing him, Macrina, while thanking God for moving her brother to visit her, tried to stretch out as far as she could as if to pay him the "honor of a bow" (ibid.). He presents her as the one in charge of their final conversation, telling stories from their family life like an historian. Gregory was moved to tears when they spoke of Basil, by this time dead, while she used their words as "a starting point for the higher philosophy" (ibid.). After their conversation he admits to "being lifted outside human nature by her words, and with the guidance of her speech, to stand inside the heavenly sanctuaries" (ibid.). It is worth including in this narrative at least part of Macrina's lengthy final prayer:

You have released us, O Lord, from the fear of death.
You have made the end of life here on earth a beginning of
**   true life for us.**
You let our bodies rest in sleep in due season and you
**   awaken them again at the sound of the last trumpet.**
You entrust to the earth our bodies of earth which you
**   fashioned with your own hands and you restore again**

what you have given, transforming with incorruptibility
and grace what is mortal and deformed in us.
You redeemed us from the curse and from sin, having
become both on our behalf.
You have crushed the heads of the serpent who had seized
us in his jaws because of the abyss of our disobedience.
You have opened up for us a path to the resurrection,
having broken down the gates of hell and reduced to
impotence the one who had power over death.
You have given to those who fear you a visible token, the
sign of the holy cross, for the destruction of the
Adversary and for the protection of our life.

Gregory was distressed at the poverty of the convent and the
lack of material means to have what he considered a fitting
funeral for his sister. However, a deaconess who knew exactly
what Macrina had decided regarding her funeral said, "You have
in your hands everything she put away. Look at her cloak, look at
the veil on her head, the worn sandals on her feet; this is her
wealth, this is her fortune. Apart from what you see there is
nothing laid by in hidden chests or chambers in reserve. She
knew only one repository for her own wealth, the treasury of
heaven..." (ibid.).

Gregory closes the account of his beloved sister's life by telling
some of the miracles worked through her intercession. He gives
a more detailed account of one of them. A soldier, his wife and
his little daughter, who suffered a serious eye ailment, once visited the monastery headed by their bother Peter. When they
decided to leave, Macrina would not permit them to do so.
Instead, she held the little girl in her arms and insisted they not
leave until she had made them a meal and they could continue
their conversation. With that, she kissed the child and, noticing
the eye infection, said, "If you do me the favor of sharing our
table with us, I will give you in return a reward to match your
courtesy" (ibid.). (How refreshing to have Gregory include this
mischievous, feminine touch into the story!) When they asked
what that might be, Macrina said she had an eye ointment which

had the power to cure the infection. After the meal the visitors left and, on the way home, recalled what Macrina had said. Suddenly they realized they had left without receiving the medicine. About to return to the monastery, the mother happened to look at her child and saw that she had already been cured. They knew then that the healing ointment had been the prayer of Macrina!

ATHANASIUS

The Invisible Bishop

St. Athanasius, bishop of Alexandria, Egypt, during the fourth century, was sometimes known as the "invisible patriarch" because he spent seventeen of his forty-five years in office (328-373 A.D.) in exile. He was born near Alexandria around 295 A.D., living seventy-eight years until his death, May 2, 373, which is still celebrated as his feast. Though little is known about his early life, some scholars speculate that his parents were wealthy and of high rank. All agree that he had a good education, evidenced by quotations from Aristotle and Plato in his earlier writings and, later, from Homer.

One author credits what he calls Athanasius' "hardness of character and a mania for absolute, cut and dried decisions" to his experiences in the last of the great persecutions. True or not, other descriptions of his personality also indicate he was a tenacious, strong-willed man. Nevertheless, St. Basil the Great was extravagant in his praise of the saint's commanding personality, describing him as resolute, versatile, resourceful, implacably honest—even with himself—and a single-minded lover of Christ. Basil claimed that though Athanasius refused to admit error in his friends while seeing little good in his enemies, he could be very generous with the latter if he saw in them his own characteristic of sticking by principle. So long as his cause was being promoted, he could also be selfless in matters involving his personal self-interest.

Regardless of what historians may conclude about him, it is certain that he was an organized and brilliantly shrewd thinker,

ATHANASIUS

using these abilities to prove his beliefs. Though his greatest achievement was his defense of the Church against the Arian heresy, the Arians were not the only recipients of his opposition. The fight against the Arians took place at the Council of Nicaea in 325 A.D., convoked by Constantine the Great. When asked to accompany his bishop, Alexander, Athanasius objected to this intrusion of civil government into Church affairs saying, "What has the Emperor to do with the Church?" This made him the first advocate of Church freedom against a Christian ruler. From then on, for years, a war of wits ensued between these two strong personalities. After the Council Constantine, wanting to reinstate Arius for political reasons, found Athanasius his sole opponent.

After Bishop Alexander died it was common knowledge that he wanted Athanasius to succeed him, but some ecclesiastics feared the ruthless energy of this young man. Nevertheless, by this time, he had been so successful in fighting the Arians that he had already won the office by popular consent before being elected to the office legally by the bishops of Lybia and Egypt. He was a master at impressing ordinary people but the stormy life he led with ecclesiastics and with the emperor read like escapades in the life of St. Paul. An exile for Christ, he was forced, at times, to hide in the tomb of his father. Fortunately, Athanasius did not suffer death at the hands of his enemies; in fact, he is one of the few "martyrs" in the Church vindicated before his death.

The see of Alexandria, at the time, was second only to Rome, thus giving Athanasius considerable influence. In addition, he was trained in administration by the well-organized and efficient Alexandrian hierarchy. One writer wryly comments that Athanasius reminded him more of the ancient Pharaohs than philosophers the way he used theology as a weapon against his opponents. He was the first Greek Father not at home in the academic atmosphere of Christian philosophy. His teachings were brilliant and orthodox, but the way he enforced his beliefs won him many enemies. Media people who capitalize on sensational trials today would not lack for material if they decided to use his story on the screen. So many complaints were lodged against

Athanasius—including bribery, sacrilegious acts and even murder—that it was impossible to track them down. Speaking in his
own defense, he cleared himself of all charges, however, sometimes even winning the emperor over. Once he talked his way out
of an accusation by protesting uninterruptedly; before sentence
could be imposed, he escaped secretly by sea. Later he turned up
again and demanded an audience with the emperor, surprising
him with his violence and impetuosity. On Athanasius' own
admission, Constantine's patience had been pushed to the limit;
he was sent to Trier, the beginning of five exiles.

God knows how to draw good out of the most unlikely circumstances and, as a result of these exiles, the whole western
world became Athanasian in belief; this, in turn, eventually
improved relations between the eastern and western empires.
After the death of Constantine, the empire was divided between
his two sons. Athanasius managed to persuade the stronger ruler
in the west to convince the weaker son in the east to readmit him
to Alexandria. This pattern of moving in and out of his episcopal see continued most of his life, with his enemies trying to
make it look like a struggle for the political power of the emper-
or and Athanasius always bringing the controversies back to a
theological level.

Athanasius did not see the Church as a sacramental institution
so much as one which sustains sacred dogma. He himself came
to be seen as the living symbol of the unconquerable Church (his
name means "doctrinal"). Though he did not write specifically
on the doctrinal authority of the Church, he often referred back
to the Nicaean council and its creed as if it were authoritative.
Because of this he created the idea of the first "ecumenical council." Anything contrary to its doctrine was considered by him to
be "godless maneuvers." Thus we have the beginnings of an
inflexible way of looking at the Church's doctrines which sometimes prevails even today.

After Constantine, the pagan emperor Julian decided that the
Church would take care of its own conflicts, paving a way for rec-
onciliation between the Arians and the followers of Athanasius.
Now under no coercion, the two factions were united further

against the pagan worship once again revived under this ruler. On this matter, Athanasius, characteristically unscrupulous and self-righteous, was adamant about making any concessions and so was banished again, comforting his followers with these words: "Do not be led astray, brethren, it is but a little cloud and it will quickly pass."

WORKS OF ATHANASIUS

So admired were the works of Athanasius that one sixth century abbot said, "If you find something of the writings of St. Athanasius and you have no paper handy, write it on your clothes." A more playful, serene side to this seemingly serious personality is found in them, especially in his "Festal Letters" and "Letter to Marcellinus" (a handbook, unique in his day, which encouraged ordinary Christians to meditate on the Psalms apart from their formal recitation), but also in others, even such a serious work as "Against the Pagans," where he describes God in the following way:

> Just as a musician, tuning his lyre and skillfully combining the bass and the sharp notes, the middle and the others, produces a single melody, so the wisdom of God, holding the universe like a lyre, draws together the things in the air with those on earth, and those in heaven with those in the air and combines the whole with the parts, linking them by his command and will, thus producing in beauty and harmony a single world and a single order within it...(Against the Pagans, #42).

The time Athanasius spent exiled in the Egyptian desert regions gave rise to many imaginative legends about him. Unlike most saints, his holiness was not attributed to any miracles, but rather, to the very character of his life: he sacrificed his peace, security, reputation, friends—everything—for God. The influence he had received from the school of thought found in Clement of

Alexandria and Origen (though more from eastern theology after Nicaea) gave him most of his ideas on asceticism. These are evidenced in the kind of monasticism found in his famous book, **The Life of St. Anthony**, in which certain features of Christian salvation became standard for later saints, particularly monastic saints: the ability to be converted; the ladder-like quality of sanctity (that is, one moves "upward" through the gradual practice of the virtues as well as risking a "fall" through pride the higher one proceeds); the recognized need for depending on Christ because of our own lack of resources; the need to do good things for Christ as he does them for us; the identification of the saint with Christ, i.e. we become Christ.

TEACHINGS

Athanasius was not a systematic theologian and, since he was not a philosopher, he had no interest in speculative theology either. Everything he taught stemmed resolutely from one principle: the redemption, especially Christ's death on the cross. The center of his faith was the incarnation. In his view, the Arians, who denied the divine nature of Christ, betrayed everything the Church stood for from the beginning. It is no wonder his greatest work, on the incarnation, is called the "Golden Treatise." Theologians, returning to the sources, find in it a theology more compatible with modern thought than theologies of later centuries. The term "supernatural" was foreign to Athanasius. For him, our "original state" was not one of nature without grace for, coming from God, it was already graced. Human nature had a capacity for perfection and a destiny to correspond with it. For this reason, though our graced state could be impaired, it could never be lost in an absolute sense. Sin, in his thought, was a movement toward non-existence which necessitated the restoration of sinners to their original movement: advancing toward God.

According to Athanasius, the presence of the Word in a human body took care of this restoration. Jesus' death meant that death in human beings had run its full course and so ceased to have its force in human life; Christ's resurrection spelled victory over death. Origen saw our destiny as a return to our original condition, but Athanasius went a step further and said the incarnation brought us to a greater destiny than we could have realized: becoming sons and daughters of the Father. With Irenaeus and the eastern Fathers he saw sanctification as deification. This idea of humans moving upward from a less developed stage to a more developed stage bears striking similarity to current scientific and psychological thought.

Another point in which Athanasius resonates with moderns more than with the ancient Christian writers is his emphasis on God as intimately immanent, present within our world rather than transcendent and remote from it. Unlike the Arians, he declared that "all things are capable of bearing God's absolute hand" (**Defence of the Nicaean Definition,** #8), without, in this matter, the necessity of Christ's mediation. Though Christ was the unique revelation of God, Athanasius held strongly to the integrity of Jesus' humanity for it was his belief that human nature is a suitable instrument of divinity. The way Christ paved the way for our divinization can be seen in this interesting passage from his "Golden Treatise":

> ...the Lord came to overthrow the devil, purify the air, and open for us the way up to heaven, as the Apostle said, "through the veil, that is, his flesh." This had to be effected by death, and by what other death would these things have been accomplished save by that which takes place in the air, I mean the cross? For only he who expires on the cross dies in the air. So it was right for the Lord to endure it. For being raised up in this way, he cleared the air from the wiles of the devil and all demons...(**On the Incarnation,** #25).

BASIL THE GREAT

The Great Cappadocian

Those of us who have experienced the novelty of biting into a fortune cookie will be interested to know a similar custom exists in the eastern rite of Roman Catholic and Orthodox churches. A "St. Basil's Cake" is blessed and served January 1 on the patronal feast of their favorite saint. Before the cake is baked, a coin is blended into the batter and whoever eats into the piece containing the coin must sponsor the party for his feast the next year. Who is this man whose life is celebrated in this delightful way and whose anniversary of death attracted numerous noted theologians to Toronto, Canada, for a symposium June 10-16, 1979, this man who merited an Apostolic letter from Pope John Paul II that same year?

St. Basil was born 329 or 330 A.D., around the same time St. Athanasius was made a bishop and the location of the empire was shifted from Rome to Constantinople. This placed him in the center of most theological and ecclesiastical interest at the time. Through his grandparents he was brought into contact with the church of the martyrs at a very early age. His maternal grandfather lost both his life and property during the persecution of Diocletian; his paternal grandparents barely escaped the persecution of Maximinus II by fleeing to the mountainous region of Pontus where they endured severe hardships and endless wanderings. Basil's immediate family was of a noble and wealthy class. His father, a bishop, enjoyed, as did bishops at the time, public esteem and influence in their area of jurisdiction. His mother bore ten children, five girls and five boys, one of whom died in infancy and three of whom became bishops: Basil, Gregory of Nyssa and Peter of Sebaste. When their father died, Basil's mother, Emmelia, joined his oldest sister in the desert where they led a monastic life. The latter, known as St. Macrina the Younger, was considered a model of the ascetic life.

Basil received his elementary schooling from his father, a rhetorician in Pontus, and his higher education in the schools of rhetoric at Caesarea, at Constantinople and, after 351, at Athens. Caesarea at this time was the literary and civil capital of Asia Minor. With such a background, he received the broadest liberal education of his day. It was during this period that Basil met Gregory of Nazianzus who became a lifelong friend. One author claims Gregory saved Basil from the other students by outwitting them in the pranks we associate with freshman initiation. The two friends, together with Basil's blood brother, Gregory of Nyssa, became such famous theologians that today they are commonly identified by a single term, "The Cappadocians," so-named because they lived in the area known as "Cappadocia."

In 356 A.D. Basil went back to Caesarea to teach, but soon after had a spiritual experience which impelled him to give his life to God alone.

> **I had wasted much time on follies and spent nearly all my youth in vain labors, and devotion to the teachings of a wisdom that God had made foolish (1 Cor. 1:20). Suddenly I awoke as out of a deep sleep. I beheld the wonderful light of the Gospel truth, and I recognized the nothingness of the wisdom of the princes of this world that was come to naught (1 Cor. 2:6). I shed a flood of tears over my wretched life, and I prayed for a guide who might form in me the principles of piety (Letter 223, 2).**

This experience, together with his family's tradition and, later, his impression of the ascetics who lived in the deserts of Egypt, especially Eustatius of Sebaste, all directed him toward monastic life. It is believed that his sister Macrina, concerned about the effect worldly success might have on her gifted brother, an excellent rhetorician, was also very influential in this decision.

After his spiritual awakening, Basil was baptized and then journeyed through Egypt, Palestine, Syria and Mesopotamia, visiting the most famous desert ascetics. He said: "I admired their continence in living, and their endurance in toil. I was amazed by their persistence in prayer and their triumph over sleep... ...I prayed that I, too, as far as in me lay, might imitate them." Egypt was a natural place for him to settle; it was the cradle of the eremetical life founded by St. Anthony and the semi-eremitical life originated by Pachomius. This was a combination well suited to Basil who desired an ascetical life involving individual effort as well as a corporate stable monastic life. However, in 358 he founded a monastic retreat nearer his home in a forest solitude on the banks of the Iris river where Gregory of Nazianzus collaborated with him in writing the **Philocalia**, an anthology of Origen's works. In a letter in which Basil urged Gregory to join him he describes this place as an idyllic hermitage of peace and contentment.

After he founded a number of monasteries, he was persuaded to become a priest by Eusebius, bishop of Caesarea, who wanted to make use of his talents. He was ordained in 364 A.D. and after Eusebius' death (370), succeeded him as metropolitan of Cappadocia. As bishop, Basil was first of all a Christian monk— an ascetic and a theologian. He tried to restore the life and vigor of the original Christian community as found in the "Acts of the Apostles." Though he enforced neglected ecclesiastical regulations, he always tried to give intelligible reasons for whatever he did. He consulted with his bishops and he often took the blame when complaints were raised in his diocese. Because Church unity was so important to him, he required from his bishops an ecumenical outlook. For Basil, unity already exists in the Church, but its members must make it visible. He urged the laity, especially profiteers and the rich, to be generous to the poor, particularly during the great famine in 368 A.D. Around a central monastery he established so many charitable institutions—hospitals, hospices for strangers, homes for the poor and so on—that these places came to be known as "new city" within the city. He set a precedent in what we would call "homiletics" for he initiated the formal sermon in Greek according to rules of rhetoric.

The Arian controversy was not over in Basil's day. Once his mettle was tested by Emperor Valens who threatened him with confiscation and exile if he did not sign a written statement supporting the Arian cause. St. Gregory of Nazianzus recorded his reply: "The confiscation of goods does not harm one who has nothing... Exile I do not know, for I am bound to no one place... for the whole world is of God, whose dweller and sojourner I am" (Oration, 43, 49). Soon after his ordination he wrote his **Books Against Eunomius** and joined Eusebius in the doctrinal struggle. In his theology, Basil concentrated not only on the individuality of the persons of the Trinity, but on their mutuality. His work, **On the Holy Spirit**, helped in the formulation of a statement made on the subject at the Council of Constantinople in 381 A.D. In it, he refuted not only Arianism but Macedonianism which did not give equality to the Holy Spirit. Doctrinally he went beyond Athanasius' teachings but he did not drive a point to death as the latter was inclined to do. He was more discreet.

In regard to evil, Basil was Greek, dualistic in thought. He did not see this world as evil but as an inducement to evil. For example, though he was aware of the dangers of classical literature, he did not, for that reason, ignore its treasures. His view, which can be found in his educational treatise, "Exhortation to Youths as to How They Shall Best Profit by the Writers of Pagan Authors," was selectivity: take the good from it and dispose of the rest. He stressed community life more than most theologians up to this time. Monastic life, for him, was fundamentally a life in common where all served one another and each was helped and developed by the other. Prayer, in his thought, required a rhythmic pattern; this pattern was evidenced in his monasteries. At community meetings, opinions and problems were aired freely. The central activity of the monastery was a study of Sacred Scripture, especially St. Paul and the Synoptics: Matthew, Mark and Luke.

OTHER WORKS OF BASIL

In addition to his dogmatic works, which reflect the controversies of his day, Basil is credited for thirteen writings under the single title, **Asceticism**. His **Moralia**, though it concerns general duties, is also strongly geared toward the ascetical aspects of Christian living. In it he is down-to-earth, simple and precise. As he was in touch with the church of the martyrs, so also his preface to this book shows he was in touch with the church of sinners: he bemoans the state of many churches divided against each other. His later works include two monastic rules: **Detailed Rules** which discusses the principles of monastic life and **Short Rules** which makes practical application of these principles on a day-to-day basis. It was these rules which earned for him the title, "Lawgiver of Greek Monasticism"; they also became references for later monastic lawgivers, notably Cassian and St. Benedict.

In addition to these writings, Basil is credited with many homilies and sermons. Nine homilies, under the joint title, **In Hexameron**, have become more famous than the rest. They deal with the account of creation in Genesis. He also wrote some homilies on the Psalms, intended for the purpose of edification and moral application more than for explaining their content. Finally, the **Letters of Basil** are a copious (in one edition, 365 of them) and valuable source of information for the history of the eastern Church in the fourth century. These include letters of friendship, recommendation, consolation, canonical and liturgical matters. Of the latter, letter 207 gives us a description of the ancient vigil services and letter 93 recommends daily communion. Probably the most widely-known work attributed to him is the so-called "Liturgy of St. Basil," though it is not certain whether he actually formulated it or not. This liturgy goes back historically to him nevertheless.

In our day, characterized by the extremes of wealth and poverty, Basil's words to those who have still applies:

Come then; dispose of your wealth in various directions...Do not press heavily on necessity and sell for

great prices. Do not wait for a famine before you open your barns. ...Watch not for a time of want for gold's sake, for public scarcity to promote your private profit. Drive not a huckster's bargain out of the troubles of humankind. Make not God's wrathful visitation an opportunity for abundance (Homily VI, on Lk. 12:18).

GREGORY OF NAZIANZUS

Saint of Unfulfilled Dreams

Can one really be unfulfilled and still beome a saint? Yes, if we can judge by the life of St. Gregory of Nazianzus. Born around 329 A.D. near Arianzus in Cappadocia, he, like St. Basil the Great, was educated at home by wealthy, aristocratic parents. He had a brother, Caesarius, and a sister, Gorgonia, both of whom preceded him in death. His mother, Noona, had much influence in Gregory's earliest training, consecrating him to God, as we read in his writings, before his birth. She is credited also with the conversion of Gregory's father from a sect called the Hypsistians, which combined Christian, Jewish and pagan elements.

From Arianzus, Gregory traveled to Caesarea of both Cappadocia and Palestine, and to Alexandria and Athens. He was in Alexandria during the time St. Athanasius was bishop but, since the two never met, it is assumed Athanasius was on one of his exiles. Gregory's great admiration for the bishop can be found in one of his orations (#21): "In praising Athanasius, I shall be praising virtue. To speak of him and to praise virtue are identical, because he had, or, to speak more truly, has embraced virtue in its entirety."

Gregory was enthusiastic about the academic world found in Athens but disappointed in the superficiality of its social life. It is possible that a dream he had (of his mother saving him in a storm at sea) while en route to Athens persuaded him to promise to be baptized and contributed as well to his avoidance of the evils of the day. From Athens (around 360 A.D.), he went home, occasionally spending time in Basil's monastic settlement in Pontus. It was at this time that the two men compiled their Christological work called **Philocalia**, based on the writings of Origen.

While events in Gregory's life seemed always to propel him into constant activity and positions of prominence in the Church of his day, his heart yearned, even as a student, for the peace and quiet of monastic life. His, however, were disquieting times. The emperor of Constantinople, Julian the Apostate, had gone to school with Gregory, but later broke with the Church altogether. Pressure was brought to bear on Nazianzus where Gregory's father was the bishop. In 361, at the insistence of the people, his aged father ordained him to the priesthood against his will. After this incident, Gregory preached his famous oration on the priesthood. It reveals his desire to justify why he did not pursue the monastic vocation, pushed as he was, from active life to contemplative life and back again. As one scholar describes Gregory's vacillation, his entire career became a "succession of flights from and returns to the world." Another author implies that Gregory always accepted positions from a sense of duty but then was unable to fulfill them, lacking the expertise.

It was probably at Caesarea of Cappadocia that Gregory first met Basil, but in Athens their friendship was cemented: "We were contained by Athens, like two branches of some river-stream, for after leaving the common fountain of our fatherland, we had been separated in our varying pursuit of culture, and were now again united by the impulsion of God no less than by our own agreement" (Or. 42). About two or three years after Gregory was ordained, Eusebius ordained Basil against his will. Scholars delight in comparing the two men. Some make much of their friendship, others of their quarrels. Basil was of a fiery temperament. Gregory was a mild and gentle person. However, as one author points out, Gregory's letters to Basil were not entirely non-assertive; rather, they were filled with "warm words and cold logic."

Of the two, Gregory was probably the more magnanimous; he, unlike Basil, was aware of his own faults: "I have always preferred the great Basil to myself, though he was of the contrary opinion; and so I do now, not less for truth's sake than for friendship's. This is the reason why I have given his letters the first place and my own the second. For I hope we two will always be coupled together; and also I would supply others with an example of modesty and submission" (Letter 53). At times, Gregory was the mediator in the strained relations Basil had with the civil and religious rulers of his time.

From the conflicting reports given by various scholars about their abilities, one could conclude the comparisons depend largely on the writer's own particular bent. A more balanced view might credit Basil as being the more able administrator, Gregory the superior writer and orator. The latter's chief success was his eloquence. Honored with the title, "The Christian Demosthenes," his oratory even drew St. Jerome, who came all the way from Syria just to hear him speak. Perhaps Gregory's sense of humor and lightheartedness are traits most hidden from us by historians. They can be seen in this passage of a letter to a farmer-friend:

> I did not ask you for bread, just as I would not ask for water from the inhabitants of Ostracine. But if I were to ask for vegetables from a man of Ozizala it were no strange thing, nor too great a strain on friendship; for you have plenty of them, and we a great dearth. I beg you then to send me some vegetables, plenty of them, and the best quality, or as many as you can (for even small things are great to the poor); for I am going to receive the great Basil, and you, who have had experience of him full and philosophical, would not like to know him hungry and irritated (Letter 25).

Shortly after the Arian emperor Valens succeeded Julian, a dispute arose concerning the claim of an Arian bishop over a certain territory in Cappadocia. In order to secure his own rights, Basil, by then the archbishop of Caesarea, created some other bishoprics and appointed Gregory head over a very small, miserable place. This resulted in a falling out in their friendship for a time. In 379 Theodosius, a Christian ruler, called on Gregory to rehabilitate the Church of Constantinople, by this time practically extinct after a forty years' succession of Arian bishops. It was during his stay here that Gregory preached his famous "Five Orations." In 382 the emperor convened the Council of Constantinople (the second ecumenical). One of the first acts of the Fathers of the Council was to make Gregory archbishop of Sancta Sophia. Shortly after that he was voted in as president of the Council. His unsuccessful attempts to heal a schism in the Church of Antioch caused him to resign, and he retired to Arianzus where he devoted himself to a life of prayer and asceticism until he died in 389 or 390 A.D.

Though he did not write any biblical commentaries or dogmatic treatises, five of his forty-five theological orations, delivered against the Eunomians and the Macedonians,* won for him the title, which he alone among the Fathers of the Church shared with St. John the Evangelist, "THE Theologian" (meaning the "divine theologian"). His funeral oration for Basil gives us a most interesting account of university life at Athens in the middle of the fourth century. He was strong in his teaching on the Trinity, going so far as to say against the Arians, "To curtail the Trinity even a little is equivalent to destroying it completely, as though one were to make assault on the doctrine of God altogether and with uncovered head" (Or. 5, 11). He gave more emphasis to the Holy Spirit than St. Basil dared, saying the work of the Holy Spirit was to free us from our earthly fetters so that we could ultimately become wholly divine.

Other than his orations, the greatest works we possess today are his letters (243 of them) and 507 poems. He seems to have been the first Greek author who collected and published his own letters. It is claimed that much of his writing is simply prose

---

*The Eunomians denied Christ's equality with the Father and said God's essence could be known through reason alone. The Macedonians claimed the Holy Spirit was inferior to the Father and Son.

turned into poetry. Note, for example, the way he expresses himself in this letter to Basil's brother, Gregory of Nyssa:

> **You are distressed by your travels, and think yourself unsteady, like a stick carried along by a stream. But, my dear friend, you must not let yourself feel so at all. For the travels of the stick are involuntary, but your course is ordained by God, and your stability is in doing good to others, even though you are not fixed to a place; unless indeed one ought to find fault with the sun for going about the world scattering its rays and giving life to all things on which it shines; or, while praising the fixed stars, one would revile the planets whose very wandering is harmonious (Letter 81).**

His perfection in form and style surpassed all the Christian rhetoricians of his time. He regarded rhetoric as a "weapon of virtue" in the hands of an honest person and bitterly denounced the Emperor Julian the Apostate for trying "to obstruct our education." His poems were not only intended as propaganda against heresies, but to compensate for contemporary pagan writings which he felt were not suitable for Christians.

Perhaps this man, so inept in administration, was more heart than head. In this passage taken from "The Second Oration on Easter," in which Gregory describes God's work in the new creation, ourselves, we get a little insight into the way he might have felt about the ups and downs of his life:

> **For a crooked sapling will not bear a sudden bending the other way, or violence from the hand that would straighten it, but will be more quickly broken than straightened; and a horse of a hot temper and above a certain age will not endure the tyranny of the bit without some coaxing and encouragement (#12).**

GREGORY OF NYSSA

Father of Mysticism

Gregory of Nyssa, one of the Cappadocians and brother of St. Basil, was born in Caesarea, the capital of Cappadocia about 335 or 336 A.D. His family had wealth and distinction and were conspicuously Christian, no mean feat in a day when, as we learned in the life of Basil, his grandparents suffered during the early persecutions. After his father died, Gregory and his four brothers and five sisters were raised by their grandmother Macrina and mother Emmelia, who were strict in bringing them up as Christians. His oldest sister, also named Macrina, shared in this upbringing and had great influence over him in religious matters.

Gregory was the third son and one of the youngest in the family. Three sons became bishops. Some authors speculate that he was educated at home because he was not strong in health. By his own admission, it was Basil, his senior by several years, who took care of his intellectual development after the father's death. Gregory speaks of him as his "revered master." He did not have the benefit of foreign travel or residence in Athens as had Basil and perhaps this is one reason he tended to be more shy and retiring in disposition. For years he stayed at home without choosing a profession, living on his share of the paternal property and educating himself through his own disciplined study program.

He remained unbaptized for years. His first inducement to become a Christian came as the result of a dream or vision. At

his mother's request, he had gone unwillingly to a religious ceremony in honor of the Forty Christian Martyrs. Tired by his journey and the long service he fell asleep in the garden. He
dreamed that the martyrs appeared to him and, reproaching
him for his indifference, beat him with rods. On awaking he was
filled with remorse and hastened to make amends, pleading for
mercy and forgiveness. Under this influence he consented to
assume the office of reader in the church. It is from this that historians surmise he became a Christian. Because he felt he was
unfit, Gregory left the office soon after, though others say he
was simply a product of his times and, because of his love for
eloquence, became a rhetorician instead. Basil and Gregory of
Nazianzus took him to task for this, the latter accusing him of
being influenced by vanity and a desire for public display rather
than conscientious scruples.

Some historians say Gregory was married to the sister of
Gregory of Nazianzus. This tradition is based on two obscure
passages in his writings. The tradition is so strong among scholars that sometimes his marriage is given as proof for the non-
celibacy of bishops at that time. Other scholars say his writings
only allude to the possibility of his marriage and, in fact, some
writings seem to indicate he was not married at all. No letter to
such a wife can be found in his writings. We do know his greatest ascetical work, **On Virginity**, the fruit of his stay in Basil's
monastery, extols virginity as the foundation of all other virtues.

Through the persuasion of his sister Macrina and after much
struggle, Gregory retired to Basil's solitude in Pontus and radi-
cally altered his life-style. It was here that he developed a great
love for nature:

> ...look only at an ear of corn, at the germinating of some
> plant, at a ripe bunch of grapes, at the beauty of early
> autumn...at the springs of the lower ground bursting
> from its flanks in streams like milk, and running in
> rivers through the glens...and how can the eye of reason
> fail to find in them all that our education for Reality
> requires? (On Infants' Early Deaths).

In solitude he devoted himself to a study of Scripture and the works of Origen. When Basil was called out of his retirement by Eusebius, bishop of Caesarea, to repel Arian factions, he obliged Gregory, in spite of his protestations, to serve as bishop of Nyssa, a small town west of Cappadocia. Basil, when reproached for giving his brother such a small see, replied that he did not wish him to receive distinction from the name of a powerful see, but, rather, have a see upon which he could confer distinction.

One writer, while declaring Gregory was not cut out to be a bishop, called him "the most versatile theologian of the century" and credited him with evolving a new theory of monastic life and mystical piety which surpassed Basil's. Some of his personal characteristics are revealed in a letter he unwittingly forged in order to effect a reconciliation between Basil and a relative bishop. When Basil discovered what his brother had done, the breach only widened, though a reconciliation eventually did take place. Being a bishop caused much anguish for Gregory who was more fitted for studious retirement and monastic calm than for controversies which did not end with the pen. His enthusiasm for the faith, for example, on the subjects of the Trinity and the Incarnation, brought upon him great hostility from the Arians and the Sabellians.

His whole life at Nyssa, in fact, was a series of persecutions. Certain Arian bishops even brought up a charge of uncanonical irregularity in his ordination. He was also charged, by a staff member of the emperor, of misusing Church funds. When Gregory was unable to attend the synod of Ancyra, fatigued by the journey and his anxiety of mind, Basil came to his rescue, writing a letter apologizing for his absence and summoning another synod of Cappadocian bishops in order to prove the falsehood of the embezzlement charges. This did not satisfy his enemies, however, and another synod took place in Nyssa itself. When Gregory refused to attend, he was denounced and deposed from his bishopric. In consequence, the emperor banished him in 376 A.D. He went to Selucia, but still pursued by his enemies, he was subjected to much bodily discomfort simply from the constant necessity of changing residences. In letters from his friend

Gregory of Nazianzus we learn how much suffering he had to bear and that his sensitivity led him to despondency. When Emperor Valens was killed in 378, Gregory was returned to Nyssa through the efforts of St. Ambrose who was a friend of the new emperor, Gratian.

But that was not the end. His brother Basil died, soon to be followed by Macrina who helped him as teacher right to the end. On her deathbed she confirmed his faith in the resurrection of the dead and lovingly reproved him for the distress he was feeling about her departure (**Dialogue with Macrina**). Later, Gregory took the bishopric vacated by Basil and his life became more prominent. The people of Ibera in Pontus were so strong in their wishes to have him as their bishop that only a military intervention subdued them. He was one of the chief prelates at the synod of Antioch which chose him to visit and reform the Church in Arabia and Babylon.

He was greatly esteemed by Emperor Theodosius who provided him with a carriage when he went on trips. A confidential advisor to those in government, Gregory was said also to have been one of the most influential theologians opposing the Eunomians at the Council of Constantinople in 381 A.D. He gave the inaugural address as well as the funeral oration for Meletius of Antioch, the first president of the Council. He was funeral orator for the infant Princess Pulcheria and, later, of the Empress herself. Scarcely anything is known of Gregory's death (probably in 395 or 394 A.D.) except that he had reached the heights foretold by Basil, for, as an authority in theological matters, he was considered, by the rulers and people, second to none.

TEACHINGS

Some of Gregory's important writings were dogmatic: four treatises against Eunomius, three on the Trinity and **The Great Catechism**, which instructs teachers to use their opponent's view as a point from which to proceed toward refutation. One of his works was meant to complete and to correct some of the

misunderstandings about Basil's homilies on creation, the
Hexaemeron. Also available for our reading are many orations
and sermons, both liturgical and moral. The letters still in existence give an idea of his diverse interests and contacts. From one
of them we see the dim view he took of pilgrimages:

> **Change of place does not effect any drawing nearer to
> God, but wherever you may be, God will come to you if
> the chambers of your heart be found of such a sort that
> he can dwell in you and walk in you. But if you keep your
> inner self full of wicked thoughts, even if you were on
> Golgotha, even if you were on the Mount of Olives, even
> if you stood on the memorial rock of the Resurrection,
> you will be as far away from receiving Christ into yourself
> as one who has not even begun to confess him.
> Therefore, my beloved friend, counsel the brethren to be
> absent from the body to go out to our Lord, rather than
> to be absent from Cappadocia to go to Palestine (On
> Pilgrimages).**

His greatest works, however, are those on asceticism and mysticism. These won for him the title, "Father of Mysticism." Of
these, the most important are **On Virginity, The Life of Moses,
The Lord's Prayer** and **The Beatitudes.** If we compare him with
the other Cappadocians, he was neither an able legislator and
administrator like Basil nor a brilliant preacher and poet like
Gregory of Nazianzus. However, he surpasses both as a speculative theologian, writer and mystic. He was the first theologian to
describe the spiritual life as an "ascent," the first to give us precise terminology describing the mystical experience of ecstasy.
He is known as the founder of "apophatic" theology which
means, basically, that we know God most when we know him the
least. In other words, the closer we come to God the more we
realize how unknowable he really is; he is luminous darkness
much the same way as a bright light blinds us. Two phrases
taken from **The Life of Moses** describe it in Gregory's own
words: "Moses' vision of God began with light; afterward God

spoke to him in a cloud. But when Moses rose higher and became more perfect, he saw God in the darkness"; and "The true vision and the true knowledge of what we seek consists precisely in not seeing..."

One scholar has called him a "discreet psychologist" in dealing with the problems of human beings, and moderns might be surprised to find how close to them he is in his teaching on perfection. Contrary to much of what we have been taught, Gregory did not see perfection as a goal to be achieved but rather, "...human perfection consists precisely in the constant growth in the good" (LOM). He is close to current theologians in his views on original sin as well. He did not see it as an accidental thing or extraordinary but, rather, as a necessary thing, a consequence of the mixed nature of our humanity: body and spirit. Children, according to him, come into the world, not with actual sins, but with forgotten sins, just as those who are baptized are re-born with forgiven sins.

He believed all of creation was completed before the six days as recounted in Scripture. This belief, known as "simultaneous creation," included us, somewhat the way we express events which happened before we were born, "We were still in the mind of God." For Gregory, nevertheless, this was real existence. He reminds us of Irenaeus in his allusion to Mary, the Mother of God, as the "second Eve" and in his firm belief in the restoration of all things in God. Further, this belief was not a cold proposition, however, but a living experience. He simply could not imagine any creatures being eternally estranged from God. He saw the end times as those when every creature would intone a chant of thanksgiving to God, when even the "inventor of evil" would be healed.

As for human beings, Gregory taught that heaven could only be attained by those who had prepared themselves for it by a battle against sin. When purification had been reached, then we would pass without any effort into heaven. His reasoning was that if God is in heaven and we adhere to God it necessarily follows that we are where God is because we are united to him. Thus, we can have heaven on earth!

JOHN CHRYSOSTOM

The Golden Mouth

"Bless me! What wonderful women there are among the Christians!" Such was the praise lavished on St. John Chrysostom's mother, Anthusa, by one of his pagan teachers. Of noble and wealthy parentage, John and his older sister received their early education from their mother who was widowed when she was only twenty, her son a mere infant. It is uncertain whether his father, Secundus, was a Christian, but his mother most certainly was. The only great Father of the school of Antioch, John was born in that city. Most authors place his birthdate between 344-354 A.D. though very little is known about this event despite the fact that his biography has been written more often by scholars than that of any other Christian writer.

Already at the age of eighteen, after some training with famous philosophers and rhetoricians, John was described by the historian Palladius as "a man of intellect" who "delighted in divine learning." He was brought to the attention of Meletius, bishop of Antioch, and admitted to baptism and, three years later, advanced to the office of reader. During his time with the bishop, he was schooled in theology by Diodore of Tarsus. After the completion of studies in law, he was so upset by the practice of taking legal fees for, as he saw it, making a worse cause seem like a better cause that he felt he was taking "Satan's wages" and left the profession for an ascetic life instead.

111

He wanted to go to a monastery, but his mother pleaded she did not want to be widowed again. Consequently, he turned his home into a monastery instead. Though his former associates at the bar found him unsociable and morose, two of his fellow pupils joined him in the ascetic life: Maximus (afterward bishop of Seleucia) and Theodore of Mopsuestia. After his mother's death, John went into the mountainous region near his home and found an old hermit whose life he shared for four years. After that, he retired to a cave, overdoing his bodily austerities to such an extent that ill health forced him back into the mainstream of the Church's life once more.

In 381 A.D. he was ordained a deacon by Meletius and a priest in 386 by Bishop Flavian. The latter appointed him to the work of preaching in the principal church of Antioch, a duty which he discharged for twelve years. In so doing, he won for himself the title, "Golden Mouth," an honor recognizing him as the greatest Christian pulpit orator of the Greek Church. Even today, he is considered a model for preachers. It was during these happy years that he preached his most famous homilies and an interesting event took place. Since there were several bishoprics available in Syria, John persuaded his friend Basil to take one of them— under the pretext that he had already been consecrated bishop of another place. This incident instigated the writing of one of John's greatest works, **On the Priesthood**, which is a dialogue between Basil and himself on the subject. It also brings out the advantages of this timely fraud in the history of the Church.

The idyllic period as preacher ended abruptly, however, when the patriarch of Constantinople, Nectarius (who succeeded Gregory of Nazianzus), died in 397 and John was chosen against his will, to succeed him. Emperor Arcadius forced him back to the capital city through persuasions of treachery and violence. There the patriarch, Theophilus of Alexandria, was compelled to consecrate him bishop on February 26, 398 A.D. Now in charge, John began his duties by attempting to reform the city and clergy whose lives had become corrupt, and it soon became evident that his type of personality made him unfit for the work which had been enforced upon him. His sense of the dignity of the human person was too lofty to stoop to the subservient attitude required by those in power. His fiery temperament betrayed him also and, like St. Athanasius, he became offensive and inconsiderate in speech and action. Perhaps his "either/or" disposition resulted from a too intent following of his hero St. Paul. His great admiration is evidenced in his commentaries on the latter's epistles.

> **...tell me, what was the case of the blessed Paul?...Did he not experience innumerable storms of trial? And in what respect was he injured by them? Was he not crowned with victory all the more because he suffered hunger, because he was often tortured with the scourge, because he was stoned, because he was cast into the sea? (from a treatise: None can harm him who does not injure himself, 11).**

His attempts to reform clergy and laity alike were uncompromising and unrealistic. In particular, he railed against attendance at the theater (calling it the "Devil's Show") and the chariot races, saying those who attended were "eating of the devil's garbage" (Homily III, 1). Having come from the provincial capital of Antioch, he was too naive to see through the cunning and deceit found in the royal city and the type of diplomacy required in order to win over his adversaries. Despite his unstinting efforts to practice personal simplicity and despite the large sums of money he used to erect hospitals and to supply aid for the poor, opposition grew stronger. It burst into outright hatred after he had six bishops deposed for practicing simony. When Eudoxia became Empress, the fury of his enemies was strengthened for it seemed to them that all his sermons on depravity and luxury were leveled at her and her court.

Theophilus, who had resented it ever since he had been forced to consecrate him bishop, was enraged when called to the capital in 402 to answer charges made against him by the monks of the Nitrian desert at a synod presided over by John. Certain that John was at the bottom of it, Theophilus called a meeting of thirty-six bishops, all enemies of the former, with the support of Eudoxia. At this so-called "Synod at the Oak," John was condemned on twenty-nine fabricated counts. The acts of this synod are still extant. When John refused three times to appear before the episcopal court, he was declared deposed in August, 403. The emperor, Arcadius, accepted the synod's decision and exiled him to Bithynia. However, the indignation of John's flock in Constantinople and an accident (by some authors said to have been an earthquake) so frightened Eudoxia that she recalled him the next day. He re-entered the city in a triumphal procession and, in the Church of the Apostles, delivered a jubilant address, still preserved.

Two months later, however, this peaceful situation came to an abrupt halt. John's irritation came to the fore again as he complained about the noisy amusements and dances that marked a celebration for Eudoxia. Jesus' words, "You must be clever as snakes and innocent as doves" (Mt. 10:16) did not apply fully to John! His enemies connived to make his complaint look like a personal affront to the empress who, in turn, let him know she resented it. Later, John committed the final imprudence. On the feast of St. John the Baptist he began a sermon with the words: "Again Herodias raves; again she rages; again she dances; again she asks for the head of John upon a platter." His enemies regarded this sensational introduction as an allusion to the empress and resolved to secure his banishment. He was forbidden the use of any church and when he and his loyal priests gathered the catechumens for baptism on the Easter Vigil in 404, their ceremonies were interrupted by armed intervention. Five days after Pentecost, John was informed that he was to leave the city at once, which he did.

He was exiled to Cucusus in Lesser Armenia where he remained for three years. When his beloved Antiochean community began to visit him his enemies, fearing the possibility of the Church of Antioch moving to Armenia, once more were driven into action. They persuaded Arcadius to banish John to Pityus, a wild spot on the eastern end of the Black Sea. Broken by the hardships of the way and by the enforced travelling by foot in severe weather, the saint died on September 14, 407 at Comana in Pontus before reaching his destination. According to some, his last words were his usual doxology: "Glory be to God for all things. Amen." His body was brought back in solemn procession to Constantinople on January 27, 438 and interred in the Church of the Apostles. It is said that Emperor Theodosius II, a son of Eudoxia, went out to meet the funeral train, laid his face on the coffin and entreated the dead bishop to forgive his parents for their ill-advised persecution of such a holy man. John's own attitude toward suffering can be summed up in his own words:

> ...when about to perform any duty to God, look forward to manifold dangers, manifold punishments, manifold deaths; and be not surprised nor be disturbed if such things happen... For surely no one choosing to fight expects to carry off the crown without wounds! (Homily 1, Concerning the Statutes, 30).

WRITINGS OF JOHN CHRYSOSTOM

This most fruitful author among the Greek Fathers wrote numerous moral and ascetic treatises, about six hundred homilies and commentaries, occasional orations, letters, and liturgical works. Most important were his homilies (on Genesis, the Psalms, the Gospels of Matthew and John, the Acts, and the Pauline epistles, including Hebrews) and commentaries. In theory he recognized allegory as a literary form, but he seldom used it in practice. He came close to Protestant thought in seeing the Bible as the sole rule of faith, believing that reading it was the best means of promoting the Christian life. He preferred the literal sense of Scripture and put himself into the psychological state and historical situation of the biblical writer. He was, therefore, quite practical in his writings and less speculative than, for example, Sts. Athanasius and Gregory of Nyssa and, consequently, less involved in the theological controversies of the time.

John's writings cover a wide range of subjects: monastic life, virginity, baptism, priesthood, widowhood and the education of children. His fifty-five homilies on Acts contain interesting information about the manners and customs of the age. He was a wholesome contrast to his contemporary St. Augustine insofar as he laid great stress on our free will in accepting or rejecting God's grace; he believed God helps those who help themselves. Unfortunately, in using the flowery and exuberant style of the day his praise of the saints was excessive and it furthered the semi-idolatry we find around the time of the Nicene Creed. This was not true of Mary however. In the few writings we find on her, he even attributes her conduct at the wedding of Cana as undue haste in wanting a display of miraculous power from her son! Another trait found in his writing which most of us would like to erase from history, found in eight homilies, is his seeming anti-Semitism. At least one author claims, however, that his railing against the Jews was not so much against the Jews as against those Christians who were frequenting synagogues. Perhaps fear led him to unreasonable exaggeration. Let us not be guilty of the same exaggeration, condemning him for his faults and forgetting that he was, after all, the "Golden Mouth."

AMBROSE

Persuasive Diplomat

Sometimes we may tend to associate St. Ambrose with the conversion and baptism of St. Augustine so much that we neglect to think of him as a person in his own right. He is perhaps the best example we have among the Church Fathers of someone who combined in himself the worldly cleverness of a serpent with the simplicity of a dove (cf. Mt. 10:16). Or, to put it in more modern terminology, he was astute both in the ways of diplomacy and in the ways of God. This particular combination seems to have been in his genes for we find martyrs as well as state officials in his family history.

Ambrose was born, probably around 340 A.D., at Treves (also Trier) where his Greek-born father, of the same name, was prefect of the Gauls. This Father of the Western Church was the first to be born, raised and educated as a Christian. After his father's early death, his mother and his elder sister, Marcellina, and brother, Satyrus, accompanied him to Rome. Marcellina later became a nun at a ceremony presided over by Pope Liberius. In Rome, Ambrose pursued studies in law. His skill and success in this field led to his rapid advancement in the profession and soon he was appointed by Probus, governor of Liguria and Emilia, as consular over one of the provinces in the empire. Probus advised, "Go and act, not as a judge, but as a bishop." So well did Ambrose follow this advice, that it is said people began to think of him as a father rather than as a judge. They soon proved their admiration in a concrete way.

As the story goes, when the bishop of Milan died and a discussion arose regarding his replacement, a child cried out in the assembly, "Ambrose, bishop!" at which the whole group took up the chant, electing him by acclamation, though he was only a catechumen and, therefore, not canonically eligible. Ambrose did everything in his power to avoid the dignity, even, according to his biographer, Paulinus, resorting to questionable means. However, after the bishop and Emperor Valentinian ratified his election, he finally submitted to it as the will of God. He was baptized and, a week later, was consecrated bishop of Milan on December 7, 374 A.D., the date which, through the centuries, has been celebrated as his feast. He was thirty-five years old.

Immediately, upon taking office, he gave up all his worldly possessions, with the exception of a set amount for his sister, for the benefit of the needy and poor. His brother left his own work to take care of this disposition of property so that Ambrose could spend all his time studying theology and taking care of his episcopal duties. His studies included Sacred Scripture and ecclesiastical writers, especially Origen, Basil the Great and Athanasius. So acquainted with these writers did he become that St. Jerome once accused him of plagiarizing them. Ambrose's knowledge of Greek was invaluable, because he was forced by the circumstances of his election to "learn and teach at the same time, since I had no leisure to learn before" (Bk. I, **On the Duties of the Clergy**, ch. 1, 4).

Today those scandalized by the involvement of priests in what is considered "political activity" cannot have read their history books thoroughly. This is not a new phenomenon in the Church; St. Ambrose was unmistakably involved in this area of human life. After his friend Emperor Gratian died in 383, the latter's brother, Valentinian II, became ruler. He was only twelve years of age and much more under the influence of his mother Justina than her husband had been. She was an Arian. When she tried to secure one of the basilicas, Ambrose chided, "The Emperor has his palaces; let him leave the churches to the bishop." When soldiers were sent to secure one of the basilicas, Ambrose and his people stayed inside singing psalms and hymns until the military personnel left. This action sounds like something we might read in the morning paper about modern day protest movements sponsored by religious people.

Ambrose, a suave diplomat, was successful, also, in ridding Italy of heathenism. At his persuasion, a pagan altar was removed from the Senate house in Rome while Gratian was in office. Twice, during the rule of Valentinian II and Theodosius, he frustrated plans to re-install the altar. It was through his efforts against the faction of Justina that an Arian bishop was not assigned to the city of Sirmium in 381 A.D.

But Ambrose's influence was more than that of a diplomat. He also imposed Church discipline. His powers of persuasion are clearly evident in the reply given him by Valentinian I, rebuked by Ambrose for the severity of some of his regulations and other abuses, "Well, if I have offended, prescribe for me the remedies which the law of God requires." He was not the only emperor chastened by Ambrose. In 390, when Theodosius put down a sedition greatly out of proportion to the cause, resulting in the death of several thousand people, he wrote a letter forbidding the emperor from participating in the eucharistic liturgy until he acknowledged his sorrow through public penance. Theodosius complied. Though Ambrose clearly let the rulers of his day know they were in the Church, not above it (Letter 20, 19), he also acted as their friend. He was arbiter between them and other difficult rulers and he preached homilies at their funerals extolling their virtues.

At the same time, Ambrose never neglected the duties of his bishopric. In addition to his studies and devotional practices, he preached on Sundays and on great feasts. He celebrated the liturgy daily and lived a personal life of virtue: he was sympathetic, energetic, and devout. Unlike many of the Fathers of the Church during this period, Ambrose did not die a martyr nor was he exiled. When his health began to fail, according to Paulinus, Count Stilicho, convinced that Ambrose's death would bring a severe threat to Italy, persuaded the nobles of the city to ask the saint to pray for a longer life. He replied, "I have not so lived among you as to be ashamed of living and I do not fear to die, for we have a good Lord." With his arms extended in the

form of a cross for the last few hours of his life, he died on
Good Friday, 397 A.D., and was buried Easter Sunday in Milan.
Perhaps the most eloquent testimony to him can be found in the
words of his greatest protégé:

> ...he (Ambrose, by his sermons) zealously provided your
> people with the fat of your wheat, the gladness of your
> oil, and the sobering intoxication of your wine...That
> man of God received me in fatherly fashion, and as an
> exemplary bishop he welcomed my pilgrimage. I began to
> love him, at first not as a teacher of the truth, which I
> utterly despaired of finding in your Church, but as a man
> who was kindly disposed toward me (St. Augustine,
> Confessions, Bk. 5, ch. 13).

WRITINGS OF AMBROSE

Ambrose wrote on a wide variety of subjects: works on dogma,
controversial issues, exegesis (a study dealing with the interpretation of Sacred Scripture) and on asceticism. Many letters and
some hymns written by him have been preserved also. One subject which fascinated him was virginity. Others had described virginity as a renunciation and as a detachment to be practiced for
the sake of purity of heart or for the Kingdom (St. Paul, St. John
Chrysostom). St. Gregory of Nyssa saw physical virginity as an
exterior sign and support of interior virginity by which we recov-
er the image of God. For Ambrose it was a pure gift from heaven;
it made the virgin Christ's bride and resulted in all the fruitful-
ness this implies. So powerful were his words on the topic that
some mothers refused to allow their daughters to attend his sermons. Three of these sermons, as well as some additional sermon
notes, were eventually compiled into four small books for his sister Marcellina, given to her on the Feast of St. Agnes, 377 A.D.,
under the title, **Given To Love**. In it, though Ambrose asserts he
is "not against marriage," calling it "virginity's source" (#35), he
seems unable to say enough about the glories of virginity:

...your virginity stands comparison with the bees. It is industrious, modest, continent. ...modesty is ever enclosed by a wall of the spirit and is not open to seizure. Inaccessible to thieves, the garden is redolent of the vine and the olive and is bright with the rose. Piety grows like the vine, peace like the olive, virginal modesty like the rose. ...when the house is all pure, unstained by sinful conscience, your spiritual home may stand as a priestly temple built upon its cornerstone, with the Spirit dwelling in it (#40, 43, 78).

One of the first Western Fathers to use an allegorical interpretation of Sacred Scripture, Ambrose borrowed from the Greeks, particularly Origen, Philo and Basil the Great. This was appreciated by the thinkers of his time who found the literal translation of Sacred Scripture unrealistic and unworthy of God. Most of his treatises on the subject were compiled from lectures he had given to the people of Milan. Of his dogmatic works, he wrote five books titled, jointly, **Of the Christian Faith**; one book, **Of the Holy Spirit**; one, **The Mystery of the Lord's Incarnation**; and one on Penance, as well as a treatise, **On the Mysteries**, which included Baptism, Confirmation, and the Eucharist. Of all these, the first two books are the most famous.

Clearly, St. Ambrose was not as creative a thinker or writer as many of the Fathers before and during his time. However, because of his ability as a diplomat, he was probably more pastoral than some of them. Though he did not compromise the Church, he was able to heal wounds and to get others to opt for a better course of action. Consider his words in Book II of **On the Duties of the Clergy**:

It is a very great incentive to mercy to share in others' misfortunes, to help the needs of others as far as our means allow and sometimes even beyond them. For it is better for mercy's sake to take up a case or to suffer odium rather than to show hard feeling (ch. 28, 136).

And, in a **Commentary on St. Luke,** this man, who truly deserved the name "father," shows how much insight he had into the human heart:

> **Peter was sorrowful and he wept because, being a human, he had strayed. I do not find that he said anything; but, I do find that he wept. I read about his tears, but I do not read about any satisfaction. But what cannot be defended can be washed away. Tears wash clean the fault which he would have blushed to confess in words...Those are good tears which cleanse from guilt (10, 88).**

JEROME

The Irascible One

Is it possible a saint deserves such a title? For the doubtful we get a flavor of St. Jerome's cantankerous disposition in the advice he offered his opponent, Onasus of Segesta: "I will give you a hint what features to hide if you want to look your best. Show no nose upon your face and keep your mouth shut. You will then stand some chance of being counted both handsome and eloquent" (Letter 40, 2). One writer described Jerome as passionate, impulsive, egotistical and sensitive to the point of morbidity. It is difficult to recount his life because of the multitudinous events which occurred in it over relatively short periods of time.

Best known for his translation of the Bible into the Latin **Vulgate**, Jerome was born at Stridon, Italy. As is true of so many of the Fathers of the Church, his birthdate is disputed, some writers placing it at 331, others at 345 A.D. Some scholars tell us his father, Eusebius, and his mother, both Christians, died when Stridon was destroyed by the Goths in 377 A.D. Jerome's early years are better situated if we recall that Constantine the Great ruled and had initiated policies which made Christianity the state religion. It was a time when both the eastern and western emperors were Christians and the Church held its first ecumenical council in 325 at Nicaea.

Jerome's family was moderately wealthy, owning houses and slaves. We learn this in a letter to Pammachius (66, 14) in which he tells of sending his brother Paulinus to Italy after the invasion to sell some "ruinous villas" and other property inherited from his parents which had "escaped the hands of the barbarians." His brother and sister were both many years his junior. Sources tell us he also had an aunt, Castorina, and a grandmother who lived with them. As was the custom in the fourth century, Jerome was not baptized in infancy but later, in 366, by Pope Liberius. He received a good education and was a good student though, strangely, he dubbed himself an "idle boy." He became a friend of Bonosus, the son of another wealthy family, and after grammar school the two traveled to Rome where Jerome studied rhetoric and frequented the law courts with a view to improving his abilities at "persuasive speech." He liked this time of his life, saying his enthusiasm for rhetorical study and erudition was "white hot." It is for this reason and his love for minutiae perhaps that made him, to his death, a stickler for grammatical correctness. He studied the classical writers—Virgil, Terence, Cicero, Lucretius—and often quoted them in his later writings. At this period he also began the acquisition of a library.

Jerome, on his own admission, began to lead a dissolute life from which, fortunately, he was diverted by his association with some young Christians who used to visit the tombs of the martyrs. After Rome he traveled with Bonosus to Trier in Gaul where Athanasius had lived in exile (335-337). His **Life of St. Anthony** was familiar to Jerome. From these and other influences he eventually sensed a vocation to an ascetic, celibate life. He confesses the difficulty this posed, however, in what has become his most famous letter:

> **Many years ago, when for the kingdom of heaven's sake I had cut myself off from home, parents, sister, relations, and—harder still—from the dainty food to which I had been accustomed... I still could not bring myself to forego the library which I had formed for myself (Letter 22, 30).**

From Trier, he and Bonosus traveled to Aquileia where they remained for three years studying Scripture and practicing asceticism, surrounded by friends of like mind, especially Rufinus and Heoliodorus. It was during this time he became associated with

PAULA AND JEROME

forms of religious life, both eremetical and communal, male and female. Suddenly there was a break with his family. There are only allusions as to what the problem may have been, but some speculate his ascetical tendencies as well as his support of his sister taking religious vows as part of the cause. This is surmised from his complaints about the worldliness of the Christians at Stridon. Jerome resolved to go to Jerusalem as a pilgrim of Christ. Other historians attribute the ruptured family relations and his final leaving of them to Jerome's tactlessness and passionate temperament; still others say he left because of slanderous rumors made about him.

En route east, possibly around 372 A.D., Jerome contracted an illness which resulted in a stay in Antioch for a full year. During this time, he made efforts to improve his knowledge of the Greek language. He records that while being overcome with a fever he had a nightmare which portrayed preparations for his funeral:

> **Suddenly I was caught up in the spirit and dragged before the judgment seat of the Judge; here the light was so bright and those who stood around me were so radiant that I cast myself upon the ground and did not dare look up. Asked who and what I was I replied, "I am a Christian." But the One who presided said, "You lie; you are a follower of Cicero and not of Christ. For where your treasure is, there will your heart be also" (Letter 22, 30).**

The dream continued but the words above point out the gist of its meaning. A turning point in his life, Jerome determined, among other things, to abandon secular studies and to devote himself entirely to sacred studies. For the next five years he lived as a solitary in the desert east of Antioch where many hermits lived under their leader, Theodosius. From letters of this period we find the very strenuous life of asceticism he undertook and the beginnings of his work with Sacred Scripture. We also find him lamenting indulgences of the past: "How often, when I was living in the desert...did I fancy myself among the pleasures of

Rome! ...Now...where I had no companions but scorpions and wild beasts, I found myself among bevies of girls..." (Letter 22, 7).

In 379 A.D. he returned to Antioch and was ordained a priest. He attended the Council of Constantinople and, though considered a Father of the West, through his acquaintance with the two Gregorys of Nazianzus and Nyssa, he came under eastern influence. Though Gregory of Nazianzus never mentioned Jerome in his letters, Jerome claimed him "teacher." He also began to admire the writings of Origen and was so vehement in his praise of him that he later regretted it. After his stay in Constantinople he went to Rome where he enjoyed the encouragement of Pope Damasus who asked him to do various translations of Scripture, one of which was the Psalms, a revision used by the Roman Church for over eleven centuries. Unlike most of the other Fathers of the Church who wrote treatises, apologies, homilies and so on for posterity, Jerome's thought is discovered only in the numerous letters he wrote and in the translations of and commentaries on Scripture which we still have today. In addition to the **Vulgate**, his translation of the Psalms and his commentaries on Ephesians, Galatians and Job are perhaps the most famous. It was Jerome's belief that "...ignorance of the Scriptures is ignorance of Christ" (**Commentary on Isaiah,** Prologue: 24, 17).

He continued to practice asceticism and began to gather like minded people around him. It was through them that he made the acquaintance of Paula, a noble and wealthy Roman woman, who became his devoted disciple and friend for the rest of her life. She had many friends of similar station and soon they began to form a group practicing an austere communal life in the home of one of them, Marcella. Here they prayed and read the Scripture under their teacher, Jerome. From this period we have a treasury of letters on their new way of life and its practices. These years, the happiest of Jerome's life, were rudely interrupted by the death of Pope Damasus. His successor felt just the opposite about Jerome. After many recriminations on both sides, Jerome determined to leave Rome and seek refuge in Palestine. Shortly afterward he was followed by Paula and her company.

The two groups, reunited in Antioch, went on to Bethlehem where Jerome spent the rest of his life (thirty-four years).

The stay in Bethlehem is usually divided into three periods. During the first, a monastery was built for men and one for women. A church which both groups attended, and a hospice for pilgrims completed their monastic setting which basically followed the pattern founded by Pachomius. For a long time the buildings were maintained through the financial support of Paula until, finally, impoverished herself, she had to depend on the holdings of Jerome and his brother. Jerome lived in a cell surrounded by his library to which he continually made additions. He lived austerely but not with excessive severity. Unlike many of the monks of his day, he did not think uncleanliness improved piety. It was during this time that he perfected his knowledge of Hebrew through the help of a Jew who, like Nicodemus, came to him at night.

Sulpicius Severus tells us that though Jerome was in charge of the parish of Bethlehem, he felt called to study rather than pastoral work, so he left that work to other priests. Crowds of monks came to see him from all over the world. He taught young people the classics to which he returned in his later years and during the second period in Bethlehem he did his greatest work, the **Vulgate** (that is, the vernacular of the people) version of Scripture. It was translated into Latin from both the Greek and Hebrew. Jerome's work was interrupted by the invasion of the Huns, and from this period we have letters describing the great controversies. Most of these letters opposed the anti-ascetic works of Jovinian and Vigilantius and the works, but not the person of Origen, and to a quarrel between himself and Rufinus. Among other things, Rufinus criticized him for going back to the classics and also for his refutations of Origen. Jerome also became embroiled in controversy with St. Augustine who had criticized his **Commentary on the Galatians** as well as his translation of the Hebrew Scriptures. Eventually their difficulties were resolved, but at one point Jerome, typically impatient, wrote: "Send me your original letter, signed by your own hand, or else cease to attack me" (Letter 105). Many of the difficulties he had with Rufinus and Augustine were increased by the poor systems of communication at the time.

The final period at Bethlehem (405-420) was passed in the midst of privations, the loss of friends and frequent illnesses. Paula died, his eyesight failed and fugitives from Rome, after the destructions of Alaric, brought more ministerial duties. Another worry was the burning of monasteries in Bethlehem by the Pelagians. Surprisingly, Jerome only engaged in a refutation of their teachings at the prodding of others; he was milder toward them than his contemporary Augustine. In the last year of his life he was tended by a younger Paula and Melania. After his death in 420, many legends sprang up regarding the transportation of his remains from the burial place near the Grotto of the Nativity in Palestine to, for example, the Church of Santa Maria Maggiore in Rome, and other legends about miracles happening near his tomb. Because of Jerome's descriptions of eremetical life in the desert, a story about his having been attended by a lion became so firmly established that the famous artist, Albert Durer, depicted it in a painting of Jerome. As is true of other irascible ones, Jerome was well loved by those who understood him.

A READING FOR PASSION SUNDAY BY ST. JEROME

"When he was at Bethany in the house of Simon the leper." "Bethany" means "house of obedience." How, then, is the house of Simon the leper in Bethany the house of obedience? What is the Lord doing in the house of one who is leprous? He went into the house of a leper in order to cleanse him. Leper implies, not one who is a leper, but who has been leprous; he was a leper before he received the Lord, but after he received him and the jar of perfume was broken in his house, the leprosy vanished. He retains his former identity, however, in order to manifest the power of the Savior.

PAULA

Woman of the Bible

It is common knowledge that St. Jerome translated the Latin **Vulgate** which, until recent times, has been the standard version of the Bible used for centuries by ordinary Christians. What many may not be aware of is that his famous work might never have been finished had it not been for the steady and persistent prodding of Paula, a widow who lived in the fourth century. We know very little about her except what we learn from the letters of St. Jerome. (Strangely, no written responses from Paula are available to us!) We moderns would find it hard to praise another in the extravagant language Jerome uses for Paula, yet once he went so far as to call on Jesus and his saints to bear witness that what he said were not words of "adulation and flattery" but sworn testimony to the truth. He claimed she was born of the nobility on both sides of her family and lauds her further by saying:

> **And who could find a greater marvel than Paula? As among many jewels the most precious shines most brightly, and as the sun with its beams obscures and puts out the paler stars; so by her lowliness she surpassed all others in virtue and influence and, while she was least among all, was greater than all. The more she cast herself down, the more she was lifted up by Christ (quoted in Silent Voices, Sacred Lives, edited by Barbara Bowe, RSCJ and others, Paulist Press, NJ, 1992, p. 179).**

She and her husband Toxotius had four daughters—Blaesilla,

Paulina, Eustochium, Rufina—and a son, Toxotius. Women of that period spent their money and time on makeup, silken clothes, golden shoes, jewels and slaves who toted them around the city on litters. Not so Paula. After Toxotius' death, when she was thirty years old, a friend, Marcella, persuaded her to become a Christian and to join a community of women pursuing a life of prayer and charity. When Jerome was appointed to be the pope's new secretary in Rome, Marcella invited him to give some lectures on the Scriptures to the community. He, realizing how intelligent they were, urged them to study Greek and Hebrew, the original languages of the Bible. His real purpose, however, was to engage them in helping him to translate the Bible into Latin. Eventually, this project became Paula's calling.

It was in Marcella's monastery (a "church in the home" as Jerome called it) that he met Paula. This encounter was the beginning of a lifelong friendship. In the fledgling monastery, Paula donned a brown tunic and began spending her money on many charitable projects. Praising her generosity, he comments:

> **What poor man as he lay dying, was not wrapped in blankets given by her? What bedridden person was not supported with money from her purse? She would seek out such with the greatest diligence throughout the city, and would think it a misfortune were any hungry or sick person to be supported by another's food. So lavish was her charity that she robbed her children; and when her relatives remonstrated with her for doing so, she declared that she was leaving to them a better inheritance in the mercy of Christ (ibid., p. 180).**

Her daughters Blaesilla and Eustochium lived with her. Jerome took special interest in them, calling Eustochium the "first virgin of Rome." To encourage her calling, he wrote a little essay on monastic life and dedicated it to her. He called Blaesilla, by now a young widow, one of his "apprentices." Paula's family was very upset because Blaesilla refused to marry again and Eustochium refused to marry at all. They believed Paula was bewitched by Jerome and even accused her of misconduct with him.

In Rome, Jerome's increased embroilment in theological controversies led him to decide to go to the Holy Land. Paula and others, including Eustochium, followed him. This enraged Paula's family so much that they started an ugly rumor—that Blaesilla's recent and untimely death at age twenty-two was due to the practice of fasts and austerities. Paula, undeterred, was, nevertheless, devastated by the loss of her daughter. She fainted behind the catafalque at the funeral and, when she came to, wept without restraint. Jerome, to console her, wrote a letter paying tribute to the dead girl. It ended with, "This letter is being written in tears.... The sorrow and the anguish you are suffering, I am suffering too. I was her father through the mind, her master through affection" (Letter 39, 1).

In 385 A.D. the group, using donkeys as their mode of transportation, began the long journey to Palestine. Jerome wrote that, as Paula left her brother, her parents and her children, "little Toxotius stretched out his hands in supplication" and Rufina, "who was of marriageable age, besought her with silent tears to wait for her wedding." But praising Paula he added, "Nevertheless, she looked up to heaven with eyes that were dry of tears, for she had put the love of God before that of her children" (Letter 108, 9). It is interesting to note that, with almost modern psychological insight, Jerome realized she did not do this without cost: "Her inward parts were churning; she was battling with grief as if she were being torn apart limb from limb..." (ibid.). A truly graphic description!

As they traveled, Jerome pointed out and reminded his companions of the biblical associations connected with various places along the way. Paula was enthralled with each place and distributed her money to those they visited. In Jerusalem the local officials had prepared an official reception and the proconsul of Palestine put his palace at Paula's disposal. She declined. About the trip Jerome notes:

She showed such fervor and devotion in visiting the holy places that the only way you could get her away from the first she saw was by letting her hurry on to the others.

She lay prostrate before the cross and worshipped the Lord, as if she saw him hanging there. As soon as she entered the Holy Sepulchre, she kissed the stone which the Angel had rolled from the door... (Letter 108, 10).

In Jerusalem Jerome met one of his old friends, Rufinus of Aquilea, who persuaded him to visit the monasteries of Egypt. Jerome and his friends journeyed there by way of Judea. En route Paula was deeply touched by what she saw in Bethlehem, the place where she would eventually be buried. Jerome records:

With the eyes of faith she could see the child wrapped in his swaddling clothes and wailing in his crib, the Wise Men adoring their God, the star shining overhead, the Virgin Mary, the zealous foster-father, and the shepherds running there through the night to see "this word that is come to pass" (ibid.).

They also visited Jericho, Sichem, Samaria, Nazareth, Cana, Capharnaum, the lake of Galilee, Tabor and many other holy places. In Egypt, she and Jerome were more interested in visiting the birthplaces of monasticism than in the places where the Israelites wandered in the desert. The heat they encountered in Egypt convinced them they should return by way of the sea to Palestine where they finally settled in Bethlehem.

Paula used her money to establish three monasteries for women which she oversaw as well as a nearby monastery for men under Jerome's jurisdiction. Only prayer rated above study in these monasteries. Paula also built a hospice to house pilgrims, orphans, and the poor and elderly. It was soon filled to overflowing. He praised Paula for being such a hard worker. The women did their own housework and made their own clothes. In one of his letters, Jerome describes the organization and routine of Paula's monasteries. Though their work and meals were separate, the three communities joined together for "Psalm-singing and prayers." They chanted the Psalter in order six times a day.

Jerome adds that "Only on the Lord's Day did they go out to

the church, which was next to where they were living..." (**Women in the Early Church,** by Elizabeth A. Clark, Michael Glazier, Inc., Wilmington, DE, 1983, p. 135). All dressed the same and anyone whose position in life had been "high-born" was not allowed to have a maid. In regard to Paula's governance of the sisters, Jerome says she approached them all differently: "If the sister were hot-tempered, with enticements; if she were unyielding, with reproaches..." (ibid., p. 136). If she noticed a sister who was "talkative, garrulous, bold and delighting in disputes," and who did not change for the better after having been corrected, she put her in the lowest rank.

Paula's money was used to cover the cost of all the books and ancient manuscripts Jerome needed. Everyone in the monasteries engaged in a serious study of the Scriptures, with Paula and Eustochium constantly encouraging Jerome to write commentaries on various books, especially those of the New Testament. Though he had been commissioned by Pope Damasus to translate the Bible into Latin, it was really through the persuasion of this mother/daughter team, particularly at the urging of Paula, that Jerome finally completed the task of translating the entire Old Testament. He would read his translations to her and she would question, criticize and encourage further research when she felt it was needed. At one point he wryly comments:

> **If at any passage I was at a loss and frankly confessed that I was ignorant, she by no means wanted to rest content with my reply, but by fresh questions would force me to say which of the many possible meanings seemed to me the most likely (quoted in Women in the Early Church, op. cit., p. 164).**

Could it be that the old adage applies here: behind the good work of every man is found the hand of a good woman? Paula herself learned to recite all the psalms in Hebrew and also began the art of hand-copying Scripture in her monastery. Contrary to custom, Jerome dedicated many of his translations and commentaries to her and to her daughter.

By the middle of 397 A.D. the Bethlehem monasteries were in financial difficulties and Paula had given away everything she owned. This seems to have been her wish. When Jerome once reproached her for her liberality she said she prayed she would die a beggar, even being indebted to strangers for her winding sheet. At all times she subjected herself to a rigorous life. Jerome once described a rather humorous incident to point out this fact—that is, it appears humorous to us but apparently not to him! It seems that once in the extreme heat of July she was overcome by a violent fever. When she began to rally, the doctor prescribed a little wine, but she continued to drink water only. Jerome comments:

> I, on my side, secretly appealed to the blessed pope Epiphanius to admonish, nay even to compel her, to take the wine. But she, with her usual sagacity and quickness, at once perceived the stratagem, and with a smile let him see that the advice he was giving her was after all not his but mine. Not to waste more words, the blessed prelate after many exhortations left her chamber; and, when I asked him what he had accomplished, replied, "Only this: that old as I am, I have been almost persuaded to drink no more wine" (Silent Voices, Sacred Lives, op. cit., p. 184).

As she approached the end of her life, Paula was a pauper and by 403 her health was so poor that she could barely drag herself from the monastery to the church. Eustochium took care of her mother's physical needs with great tenderness during her last days. When Paula died early in 404, Jerome noted with great precision that her whole life span was fifty-six years, eight months and twenty-one days. He had lost his great inspirer, the one who calmed his temper, who had admired and spurred him on in his work. Before her burial in Bethlehem on January 26, 404, Jerome spent two nights writing a funeral oration which he dedicated to Eustochium.

In his narrative on the life of Paula, Jerome describes her funeral in great detail. He says there was no weeping at her death and, with some exaggeration, that the entire populations of the cities of Palestine attended the funeral. He comments:

> **Not a single monk lurked in the desert or lingered in his cell. Not a single virgin remained shut up in her chamber. To each and all it would have seemed a sacrilege to withhold the last tokens of respect from a woman so saintly (SVSL, op. cit., p. 189).**

Jerome then describes the bishops lifting her body on a bier and carrying it into the church. In a very touching farewell to his dear friend, he asks her to aid his "ripe old age" with her prayers and adds, "Your faith and your works unite you to Christ; thus standing in his presence you will the more readily gain what you ask" (ibid., p. 191). At the end of his eulogy he notes that he has written an inscription for her tomb so that no one will be able to forget that she was buried in Bethlehem. This was the inscription Jerome wrote:

> **Within this tomb a child of Scipio lies,**
> **A daughter of the far-famed Pauline house,**
> **A scion of the Gracchi, of the stock**
> **Of Agamemnon's self, illustrious:**
> **Here rest the lady Paula, well-beloved**
> **Of both her parents, with Eustochium**
> **For daughter; she the first of Roman dames**
> **Who hardship chose and Bethlehem for Christ**
> **(SVSL, op. cit., pp. 191-192).**

On the entrance to the tomb is another inscription:

> **Do you see a narrow tomb cut in the rock?**
> **It is the resting place of Paula,**
> **Who possesses the heavenly realms.**
> **Leaving brother, kin, Roman homeland, riches,**
> **And offspring, she lies buried in a Bethlehem cave.**
> **Here was your manger, Christ,**

And here, the kings bearing mystic gifts
To a mortal man, surrendered them to God as well
(Women in the Early Church, op. cit., pp. 212-213).

Unfortunately for us, there seems to be no trace of the tomb of Paula today. However, will she not be engraved forever in our memories as one of the great Mothers of the Church?

AUGUSTINE

The Restless Wanderer

August 28, 1986, the feast of St. Augustine of Hippo, marked the 1600th anniversary of the conversion of this great Western Father of the Church. Very often, in our attempts to re-assemble the lives of our ancestors, we are stymied by our lack of information or by a discrepancy in information, depending on who has written their biography prior to us. Once in a while, as was the case of St. Anthony of the Desert, we can rely on the history of a person as reputable as St. Athanasius. However, in the present instance, we are fortunate in having all necessary, salient information supplied by the saint himself in his fascinating autobiography, the **Confessions**. As we know, he did not try to gloss over his foibles as others often did in writing the biography of a favorite person.

He was born Aurelius Augustinus on November 13, 354 A.D. at Thagaste, a small town in northern Africa, perhaps of middle-class parents—a pagan father, Patricius, and a Christian mother, Monica. From the latter he inherited an affinity for things spiritual and intellectual. We might wish he had inherited less of his father's fiery temperament and more of his mother's tender sensibilities, but, as usual, God knew better. This combination culminated in a yearning for God which is expressed succinctly in his often-quoted, "You have made us for yourself, O God, and our heart is restless until it rests in you" (Conf. 1, 1). The seed of piety and love planted in Augustine remained present but dormant all through his studies in Madaura and at the University of Carthage, on his journeys to Rome and Milan, and through sensual and intellectual sidetracks such as dipping into Manicheism, academic skepticism and Platonic idealism. Finally, after much struggle, the prayers of his mother, the sermons of St. Ambrose, the biography of St. Anthony, Sacred Scripture—especially the epistles of St. Paul—this great man succumbed to the grace of God.

Details about the actual moment of Augustine's conversion are recorded in his **Confessions**. One day an African official told him about some contemporary monks who were living the same kind of life as St. Anthony of the Desert. He added that two mutual acquaintances had renounced promising careers to follow this way, one of them, however, leaving and returning to his former way of life. Augustine saw himself in the latter and was greatly shaken. "Suddenly I heard the voice of a boy or a girl—I know not which—coming from the neighboring house, chanting over and over again the same words, 'Take up and read! Take up and read!'" With that he resolved to follow Anthony (who had acted on the words, "If you will be perfect, go sell all that you have and give to the poor...") and accept the first words he chanced upon as a way of life for himself. His eyes fell on the middle of a sentence: "...not in rioting and drunkenness, not in chambering and impurities, not in strife and envying, but put on the Lord Jesus Christ and make no provision for the flesh and its concupiscences" (Conf. 8, 12; Rom. 13:13, 14).

Is it mere coincidence that Augustine resonated so much with the writings of St. Paul, another fiery individual? The restless wanderer was very hard on himself after his desultory life and it comes out later in son of his writings. We know, for example, that, having fathered a son out of marriage, he often rails against women to such a degree that it is obvious he is projecting on them his own weaknesses of flesh. These writings are considered sexist today. We find a similarly harsh tone in his refutations of the Manicheans whose heretical teachings he once followed. Today we would call this severe, repugnant thought "over-reactionary."

He received baptism from bishop Ambrose of Milan on Easter Sunday, 387 A.D., together with his student and best friend, Alypius, and with his son, Adeodatus. It was a radical break with his past life. He abandoned a brilliant and lucrative position as a teacher of rhetoric, sold his possessions for the benefit of the poor and devoted the rest of his life to Christ. From his **Confessions** we know he was privileged to hold his mother in his arms as she breathed her last at the age of fifty-six. Though he reported he was "stupefied with grief," the two of them had a "heavenly conversation" not unlike that of St. Benedict and his sister, St. Scholastica, before she died. After his mother's death Augustine went to Rome for a time where he wrote books in defense of Christianity against the false philosophies of the day. When he returned to Africa, he lived a contemplative life-style with two friends on an estate in Thagaste. In 391, however, he was chosen, by popular acclamation, to be a presbyter in the city of Hippo (to situate in history, he was ordained the day St. Gregory of Nazianzus died) and, in 395, he was elected bishop of the same place, where he labored for the next thirty-eight years.

Even as bishop he lived like a monk with his clergy in a house where they shared things in common. His clothing did not distinguish him from those who lived with him. This house became a seminary of theological study which educated ten future bishops and many other students for the clergy. Though women were excluded, he did found groups of religious women, one of which was presided over by his sister, a widow. Because of his innovative combination of clerical/monastic life he unintentionally (because he was not a monk) became the founder of the Augustinian order which still bears his name today. His **Rule** is one hundred and fifty years older than that of St. Benedict.

As intellectual head of northern Africa, Augustine's influence extended far beyond his diocese; he was head, doctrinally, over the entire Western Church of his time. In his last years, more gentle in spirit, he critically reviewed his earlier works in his **Corrections**. He continued on alone as bishop until he was seventy-two when one of his friends was elected to assist him. His last days were troubled by the infirmities of old age and by the Vandals who invaded his country. Ten days before he died he went to his room where he poured out his heart in tears, praying the penitential psalms which he had had pinned up on the wall over his bed so he could not forget them. His life ended with this final act of penitence. He made no will; by that time he owned nothing.

Soon after his death Hippo was destroyed by the Vandals and a few decades later the Western Roman Empire also came to an end. But the works of Augustine lived on, bearing fruit in Europe with ideas which we still claim today. He was second to none of the Fathers of the Church in both quantity and quality of Christian literature. Despite the unpopularity of his thought among modern feminists and leaders of the sexual revolution, he is considered, even today, the foremost thinker of the Western Church between the time of Tertullian and Aquinas.

WORKS OF ST. AUGUSTINE

Since it would be overwhelming to list all his books, it seems wise only to mention a few of the most important. His **Confessions**, a devotional classic second in popularity only to the **Imitation of Christ** and **Pilgrim's Progress**, is considered by some the most edifying book in all patristic literature. His philosophical works were usually in the form of a dialogue (one includes six books on the subject of music!) and his habit of philosophizing carries over, often, into his more serious theological works written later on. The latter, in general, are refutations of the Manicheans, Donatists, Pelagians and the Arians. He wrote twenty-two apologetic books, of which **The City of God** is the most important. In it he summarizes most of his theology, providing a sharp contrast between the world of paganism (Satan's city) and the world of Christianity (God's city). In the Middle Ages this book was read more often than his **Confessions**.

Much of what we know about the Manicheans (who held that matter is evil) is found in the writings of Augustine. He was well qualified for this task, having been a member of their sect for nine years. His works against the Donatists (who held that the efficacy of the sacraments depends on the personal worthiness of the minister) give us his theology on the Church and the sacra-ments. Unfortunately, the expression, "outside the Church there is no salvation" (from his **Discourse to the People of the Church at Caesarea**) was used advantageously by the Calvinists and oth-ers even to our day. His doctrines on original sin and grace can be found in his writings against the Pelagians (who exalted human effort over God's in the work of our salvation) and his works against the Arians (who denied the divinity of Christ) added to the copious writings already found in Athanasius, Gregory of Nazianzus and Gregory of Nyssa.

This is not all. Augustine wrote twelve books explaining vari-ous parts of Scripture, particularly Genesis; one hundred and twenty-four homilies on the Gospel of John, ten on the first Epistle of John and others. In addition he wrote works of a moral and catechetical nature: three hundred and ninety-six ser-mons and treatises on a wide range of subjects. Finally, his **Rule**, already mentioned, and hundreds of letters are available for our reading. In short, he wrote so much that it has become com-monplace among moderns, when discussing any theological topic, to ask, "And what did St. Augustine say about that...?"

Despite the "bad press" Augustine gets today, if we see him as a repentant sinner, timebound by a particular era of history, it is possible to hold a more indulgent view of him. In fact, some of his writings give evidence of a hidden life of mysticism. Historians sometimes say that the kernel of his thought can be found in his **Commentary on the Psalms**: "Like the hart that yearns for the running waters, so my soul longs for you, O God." In it he counsels, "Run to the fountain (of Life); long for the fountain; but do it not any way, be not satisfied with running like any ordinary animal; run 'like the hart.' ...For we find in the hart a sign of swiftness" (COTP, 41, 2). When this restless wanderer finally turned toward the Lord he did, indeed, run. Probably one of the most beautiful passages in his **Confessions** gives poignant reminder that he wished it had been sooner:

Too late have I loved you, O Beauty, so ancient and so new; too late have I loved you! Behold, you were within

me, while I was outside. ...You were with me, but I was not with you. They kept me far from you, those fair things which, if they were not in you, would not exist at all. You have called to me, and have cried out, and have shattered my deafness. You have blazed forth with light, and have shone upon me, and you have put my blindness to flight! You have sent forth fragrance, and I have drawn in my breath, and I pant after you. I have tasted you, and I hunger and thirst after you. You have touched me, and I have burned for your peace (27, 38).

EVAGRIUS PONTICUS

Maligned Monastic

Most of us have probably been tempted by the "noonday devil";
perhaps few are aware that the term was coined by a much-
maligned monk of the fourth century, Evagrius Ponticus, the son
of a chorbishop (had all episcopal powers but was limited in the
use of them) who was possibly a country priest, was born around
345 A.D. at Ibora in Pontus on the Black Sea. Ordained a reader
by St. Basil the Great or St. Gregory of Nyssa and a deacon by St.
Gregory of Nazianzus, he accompanied the latter to the Council
of Constantinople in 381 A.D. Because he was "skilled in argument against all heresies," he was requested to remain with the
Bishop of Constantinople, Nectarius, after the Council.

Unfortunately, during his stay in this great intellectual center
he became involved in a love affair with the wife of a nobleman.
Through earnest prayer and certain providential events, including a dream warning him to "watch over his soul," he went to
Jerusalem where he received spiritual direction from a Roman
woman, Melania, who eventually persuaded him to become a
monk. With her help and after a long and severe illness—one historian claims it was of a psychosomatic nature—he was finally
released of his inner turmoil. For two years he exiled himself to
the mount of Nitria in Egypt, after which he lived for fourteen
years in the "Cells," a colony of very austere hermits out in the
desert. Though he was tormented again by temptations of the

flesh as well as against faith, it was during this time that he did most of his writing and also became known for unusual gifts of "knowledge and wisdom and discernment of spirits." He died on the Feast of the Epiphany, 399 or 400 A.D.

What we know about the life of Evagrius is found in **The Lausiac History**, written by one of his students, Palladius. Unlike many early biographies written by devoted protégés, the latter, though it is evident he admired him, did not write a glowing account of his master. The reason? Evagrius's works were hidden in obscurity for years because of his connection with Origen who, at the time, was under ecclesiastical censure. In fairness to Evagrius it must be admitted that sometimes he was accused of using Origenist ideas when, in fact, he was borrowing from Clement of Alexandria. Though his chief dogmatic works do contain certain Christological errors, most of his works, especially those on prayer, do not. Today happily, Origen is considered one of the greatest Fathers of the Church and scholars, taking a second look at his followers, are now crediting Evagrius with works once wrongly attributed to others. The fact they survived under these circumstances indicates the esteem in which they were held.

Why is Evagrius so important? One author, Derwas Chitty, says he provided Christianity with a whole new vocabulary in spirituality. Thomas Merton called him one of the "fathers of Christian spirituality" because it was through him that the foundations laid by the great Fathers of the Church, especially Origen and St. Gregory of Nyssa, were brought to the east. Most scholars agree that his influence on monastic spirituality is incalculable, saying he was the "most fertile and interesting spiritual author of the Egyptian desert." Ironically, his strongest influence on monk-writers was among those who claimed to despise him or to have no connection with him. Most notable are St. Maximus, John Climacus and Cassian—the latter having a great influence on St. Benedict.

Though Evagrius wrote numerous works—including letters, a text on monastic practices, remedies for vices, a list of biblical passages which opposed various faults, and exhortation to a virgin, a treatise on evil thoughts and Scriptural commentaries—his most widely read and popular works are **Praktikos** (on ascetic practices and virtues) and the **Chapters on Prayer**. Consisting chiefly in a series of aphorisms or short sayings, these are often hard to understand because they carry more meaning than is evident on a first reading; he is the first Christian writer to tend toward abstraction. Nevertheless, his logic and the brevity of the passages help to bring his readers into meditation. Consider these:

> **Whatever you might do by way of avenging yourself on someone who has done some injustice will turn into a stumbling block for you at the time of prayer...The one who stores up injuries and resentments and yet fancies that they pray might as well draw water from a well and pour it into a cask that is full of holes...If your spirit still looks around at the time of prayer, then it does not yet pray as a monk. You are no better than someone engaged in a kind of landscape gardening...If you long to pray then avoid all that is opposed to prayer. Then when God draws near he has only to go along with you...Someone in chains cannot run. Nor can the mind that is enslaved to passion see the place of spiritual prayer...When attention seeks prayer it finds it. For if there is anything that marches in the train of attention it is prayer; and so it must be cultivated (from Chapters on Prayer, #13, 22, 43, 65, 71, 149).**

An unusual teaching of Evagrius was his vision of the universe which he saw as being totally spiritual in the beginning. He did not say matter was evil nor that God did not create it; rather, he saw it as a consequence of inattention to God (sin). The efforts we make to rectify sin, he says, do not cause matter to disappear but spiritualize it to the maximum degree. At times his writings prove him, surprisingly, a good psychologist. For example this advice against repression: "When you are tempted do not fall immediately to prayer. First utter some angry words against the one who afflicts you. The reason for this is found in the fact that your soul cannot pray purely when it is under the influence of various thoughts. By first speaking out in anger against them you confound and bring to nothing the devices of the enemy" (**Praktikos,** #42). His practicality comes out also when he suggests pitting vices against one another to overcome them; for example, "fooling" the demon of vainglory by acting as if we were being tempted by impurity (P, #58). A final example of his common sense: "It is not possible to love all the brethren to the same degree. But it is possible to associate with all in a manner that is above passion, that is to say, free of resentment and hatred" (P, #100).

The basic spiritual system created by Evagrius describes a movement upward from purity of life to purity of thought. From the outset, he claims our temptations come from the evil spirits, from our flesh, and from the world and he lists the demons which test us; they run all the way from gross carnal ones to subtle ones such as vainglory. It is from his list of "eight basic sins" that we derive our "seven capital sins." His included gluttony, impurity, love of money, sadness, anger, *acedia*, vainglory and pride. *Acedia* was the famous noonday devil which made "it seem...the day is fifty hours long" and which instilled in the heart of the monk a hatred for place, manual labor and even life itself (cf. P. #12). The virtues opposing these sins followed a special order. Faith built up fear of God, which led to resisting the impulses of passion. This, in turn, was grafted on to patience and from the exercise of all these practices, hope was born. The final result was *apatheia* which engendered charity.

More specifically, Evagrius says temptations reach us through *pathe*, which are disordered affections paralyzing the free play of the spirit in us. Exterior practices (*praktike*) of virtue and following the commandments allow the ascetic person to arrive at *apatheia*— liberation from disordered affections. Then it is possible to arrive at *gnosis*—knowledge either about created things seen in relation to God or about God himself. The latter type of knowledge was the supreme kind; it is called "theology," and, for Evagrius, to be a theologian was to be a mystic: "If you are a theologian, you will truly pray and if you pray truly you are a theologian" (COP, #60).

For these and similar thoughts, he was criticized for exalting knowledge above love. However, *apatheia* (which had degrees and could be lost) did not mean we should suppress our human feelings, but rather, that we should purify them of anything disorderly, submitting them to that which is most spiritual in us. For Evagrius, a back and forth interplay between this process of purification and contemplation was a prerequisite; true *gnosis* only began when charity finally flourished on the soil of liberated affections. He said the signs indicating we had *apatheia* were praying without distraction, peace of soul and the ability to judge oneself objectively.

Gnosis, for Evagrius, was a knowledge of the Trinity; it was also a discovery of ourselves as we are truly—made in the image of God. For him, the Self is God-in-the-self; we are the "perfect temple of God." It was this *gnosis* that constituted the supreme knowledge and it was only obtained by the highest kind of prayer which he terms, "pure prayer." Singing the psalms was a lower form of prayer which helped overcome the passions and preceded this higher form. The one who prays imageless prayer, he concedes, has the ability to do this only as a gift from God. When the person reaches this stage it is something like a blinding light, a "luminous darkness": "Blessed is the one who has arrived at blessed ignorance." He felt it was this pure prayer which made us "equal to the angels" who are "all eyes" or "all fire," because angels are pure intelligence and for him the highest kind of prayer was primarily an activity of the intellect. The lower degrees of prayer were compatible with sorrow and suffering, but in the higher degrees there were only peace, tranquillity and joy. Neither degree was compatible with disordered passions.

Evagrius' ideas may be abstract and perhaps he is a bit neglectful of Scripture and dogma. Or some readers could be led, mistakenly, into believing the spiritual life is neatly divided into categories which can be attained in a step by step procedure. In a day much later than his own, some have interpreted his writings to say that mysticism is an extraordinary experience limited to an elite group whose passions are completely subdued. But this is to read Evagrius without discrimination as well as to lose the insights he gave us. When he emerged on the scene, he gave birth to a new way of thinking about spirituality and his emphasis on prayer is certainly to our advantage. So important was the life of prayer for Evagrius that he saw it as being synonymous with the following of Christ as is evident in his reading of a famous scriptural text: "Go, sell your possessions and give to the poor, and take up your cross so that you can pray without distraction (COP, #17).

EGERIA

The Pilgrim

Journal-keeping is a popular practice today. Most often it is used as a tool for self-understanding. How, then, would you feel if someone discovered your personal journal several centuries from now and published it for public consumption? It has happened. In 1884 A.D., G. F. Gamurrini, an Italian archaeologist and historian, found the journal of a woman, Egeria, in the library of the Brotherhood of Mary in Arezzo, Italy. We might take a dim view of a similar thing happening to us and most of us would doubt such a discovery could benefit anyone. Nevertheless, her journal, which is more strictly speaking a diary, is an important document.

Written during her three-year pilgrimage through Egypt, Palestine and Syria, Egeria's diary gives us much information about geography and the religious and liturgical life of the Church in her time as well as something about the role and status of women in her day. The document, it must be admitted, though substantial in comparison to many ancient findings, is still very fragmentary. The beginning and end of it have yet to be discovered as well as a large section in the middle. Nor are we able to glean very much about the author of the work. The only thing that yields personal information for us is the conjectures we can make from the work itself. Since its initial discovery only fragments of the work have been found and they, too, add very little to our knowledge.

What then can we determine about Egeria from her diary? Very little. Even her name is disputed. The discoverer of the diary, Gamurrini, called her "St. Silvia of Aquitaine" and said the document was probably written between 381-388 A.D. However, in our own century, Dom Ferotin linked this person to a woman named "Aetheria" from Galicia in Spain. Most debate since then has centered on what form of her name was correct: Aehteria, Etheria, Echeria or Egeria. The last name has gained the most popularity.

The dates of the diary's composition have also been disputed. Though Gamurrini suggested the late fourth century, dates ranging from 363-540 have also been suggested. Recent translators claim, however, that 404-717 seems more accurate even though it supports a markedly wider time span. With so much conjecture about the author and the time the document was written, does it really reveal any substantial information about our pilgrim and about the times in which she lived? Yes, we think it does.

We know, for example, that she was on pilgrimage for several years (three years in Jerusalem alone). In order to do this, we can assume she was of high social status with money at her disposal. She traveled with an entourage and never indicates any concern for money to support her. She is received hospitably, as was the custom for dignitaries, by the local clergy who prayed and discussed the Scriptures with her. They described the places in their territory which she was visiting and took her to new places if she was not aware of them. Soldiers escorted her in dangerous places. She always expressed gratitude for this treatment but never acted surprised; nor did she question the deference shown her.

From the diary we also learn that, though she was not learned in the secular classics, Egeria was well-read in the Scriptures. She was a member of a circle of religious women who made constant reference to events in Sacred Scripture—especially the Old Testament. The fact that her pilgrimage was to biblical lands strengthens the belief that she was well-versed in the Scriptures and knew where she wanted to go.

Whenever she reached a particular site on her journey, Egeria tells us, "It was always our custom that when we had reached the place we wanted to go, first we said a prayer, then a selection from Scripture was read, then an appropriate psalm was sung, and we again said a prayer" (**The Pilgrimage of Egeria**, #10). For this customary ritual she was the one who decided what psalms and scriptural passages would be read. An interesting point to be noted in Egeria's familiarity with Scriptures is that she sees the Old and New Testaments as one continuous text. She calls Old Testament figures "saint" (for example, "Sts. Moses, Elias, Rebecca, Jacob, Rachel" and so on) and she does not attempt in her pilgrimage to retrace the steps of Jesus, though she often invokes the help of "Jesus our God" as she travels. For her Judaism is important insofar as it is grounded and continuous with the Christian faith.

Though it seems the main reason she went on her pilgrimage (as was true for many in her day) was because she felt called to do so by God, she indicates she also did so on behalf of a group of women with whom she was associated. Scholars differ on the type of life-style she lived, but more recent ones think these were devout virgins not living as an organized monastic group of religious. Rather, they were similar to the medieval canonesses of Europe whose duties were to take care of liturgical observances in the major churches. Consequently, Egeria's text concentrates chiefly on what she assumes will be of interest to them. She enjoyed a familiar, affectionate relationship with them, calling them at various times "venerable ladies, my sisters, ladies—my light." At one point she indicates her responsibility toward them by saying, "Aware that your affection would like to know what is done daily in the holy places, I certainly ought to tell you" (ibid., #24). Another motivating reason offered by one author for Egeria's travels was that she was naturally curious and liked to search out things.

The text of Egeria's document indicates she had high self-esteem and was not intimidated by any dignitaries she met along the way. She enjoyed a certain liberty accorded to women of her status and, according to one author, her personality was refreshing:

Egeria as a person is one of the liveliest and most charming individuals of the early church to come down through

her own writings... Egeria would be a delightful companion, whose wholehearted and informed search for an understanding of the church in its present existence and biblical roots would nurture the perfect spirit for such a journey (A Lost Tradition: Women Writers of the Early Church by various authors, section on Egeria by Patricia Wilson-Kastner, University Press of America, Washington, DC, 1981, p. 77).

Not only was she curious, but certain descriptions she gave indicate that she was also a sensualist. Noting all the sights, sounds, tastes and so on along the way, she comments on them (all quotations from **The Pilgrimage of Egeria**):

...we were walking along and came to a certain place where the mountains through which we were traveling opened out into an endless valley, enormous, quite level, and very beautiful (#1). Sometimes you are so close by the sea that the waves hit the feet of the animals... (#6). I do not think that I have ever seen a more beautiful territory than the land of Goshen (#9). ...from a rock flows a great stream of water, very beautiful and limpid, and of the most delicious taste (#11) ...there were ponds full of fish, of sorts I had never seen, of great size, luster, and good taste (#19).

Indeed, at one juncture, when she was describing the splendor of the gold, gems and silk curtains of some churches, she caught her own exuberance and exclaims, "But let us return to the topic!" (ibid., #25).

The diary itself is divided into two major parts. The first half deals with her journeys: first, from Mount Sinai to Horeb (the route of the ancient Israelites) and then to Jerusalem; second, from Jerusalem to Mount Nebo through Arabia and back to Jerusalem; third, after three years in Jerusalem, to Antioch into Mesopotamia, back to Antioch, on to Tarsus through Cappadocia and Galatia to Chalcedon and finally to Constantinople. In our jet age such a trip, by means of primitive transportation and often on foot, seems impossible. The second half of the document deals with her observance of people along the way and of the Jerusalem liturgy.

From the diary we get a good picture of the ecclesiastical and liturgical practices of her day. The length of the liturgical services and the rigors practiced by the faithful seem excessive to us today (for example, week-long fasts) but Egeria is careful to note that exceptions are made:

> **But one who cannot do this fasts two consecutive days during Lent: those who cannot do that eat each evening. No one demands that anyone do anything, but all do as they can. No one is praised who does more, nor is the one who does less blamed (ibid., #28).**

Would that we were so non-judgmental! In her delightful and personal way, Egeria describes other concessions made for the weaknesses of human nature: "And whatever children in this place, even those not able to walk (on Palm Sunday), are carried on their parent's shoulders, all holding branches..." (ibid., #31). And, "Because it is quite far from the gate to the great church... all the people walk very slowly so that they will not be tired from walking" (ibid., #43).

She outlines in great detail the observances of the Lenten/Paschal season, especially the "Great Week" before the Pasch. Some of them correspond remarkably to our own renewed Vigil services, especially concerning the catechumenate and the baptismal rite. Today, however, we might balk if we were the catechumens and the bishop asked our neighbors in public such questions as "Is the person of good life? Respectful to parents? Not a drunkard or liar" or even "more serious vices?" (ibid., #45). Nevertheless, today's liturgists might find Egeria's journal a handy companion!

JOHN CASSIAN

Bridge Between East and West

...this is, as it were, our first trial in the Olympic games, to extinguish the desires of the palate and the belly by the longing for perfection...For we cannot possibly scorn the gratification of food presented to us unless the mind is...entranced with the love of virtue and the delight of things celestial (Institutes, Bk. 5, Ch. 14).

This observation made in the fifth century by John Cassian would hardly be found today in the brochures of weight-loss clinics. Yet it contains a truth subscribed to quite regularly by anyone having a smattering of human psychology: we rarely deny ourselves anything good unless there is hope of a greater compensation. His works are filled with similar practical axioms. Though St. Benedict is known as "Father of the West," it was through Cassian, more than any other writer, that the monastic practices and types of organization developed in the east were first transmitted to the western world. His most important contribution in this transmission was to bring the best teachings of the eastern monks.

Very little is known about Cassian. Historians disagree about his nationality but, because he was fluent in Latin and Greek, speculate that he might have come from somewhere in the Balkans or even from Gaul. One writer, around the end of the fifth century, called him a Scythian. Scholars conclude further that the use of classical authors in his writings—Virgil, Cicero, Persius—indicates he was well-educated. Others claim he was born into a pious, affluent family and that he was privately tutored. From one of his writings we learn, incidentally, that he had a sister (**Inst.**, 11, 35). When he was about seventeen or eighteen he and a friend, Germanus, attracted to the different types of monasticism found in the Holy Land, settled in a monastery near the cave of the nativity in Bethlehem (around 383 A.D.). St. Jerome, who also lived in a monastery in Bethlehem, was known and admired by Cassian; it seems they never met.

One day an old man, Pinufius, asking to be admitted as a novice, was put into the cell of Cassian and Germanus. It was discovered later that he was the superior of a monastery in Egypt and that he had sought admittance in order to live a more simple life-style. Cassian, impressed with this incident, resolved to go to Egypt to find out why the desert produced such holy people. Before leaving (c. 385 or later), he and Germanus solemnly promised to return to Bethlehem. In Egypt, they wandered from hermitage to hermitage or from one group of monks to another, spending their days reciting psalms or sitting on mats listening to discourses or "conferences" of the hermits. It is probable they even became members of a community of hermits headed, once again, by their friend Pinufius who was presbyter at Scete. The latter, nicknamed "The Buffalo" because of his solitary spirit, assumed legendary proportions for those wishing to lead heroic lives of desert spirituality.

Eventually, convinced they could learn nothing about perfection in their former monastery comparable to the wisdom obtained in the desert, the two monks returned to Bethlehem at a propitious time to seek release from their oath. Cassian later wrote a kind of "apologia" justifying this action (**Conference** 17), stating that it was a matter of choosing between keeping the oath or keeping faith with the pursuit of the higher ideal which prompted it. This time Cassian stayed in Egypt for about ten or fifteen years. Though historical documents do not reveal the exact reason for his leaving, it is suspected he was considered tainted with the teachings of Origen, regarded as a heretic at the time. This is surmised from his interpretation of monastic life which is largely based on Evagrius, a well-known Origenist.

Cassian next went to Constantinople where he was ordained a deacon by St. John Chrysostom, whom he admired and loved as a son. For this reason the clergy, loyal to the archbishop when he was deposed by the Synod of the Oak, entrusted Cassian with bringing their protest to Rome (c. 405 A.D.). Once there, he was ordained a priest and stayed for ten years, becoming a friend of the future Pope St. Leo. He went to Provence around 410 A.D. where he established two monasteries at Marseilles—one for men (St. Victor) and one for women. By then he was considered an authority on Egyptian monasticism and was asked by the Bishop of Apt to give conferences on the subject. These discourses, based on what he had heard in the desert, were concretized later in his most famous writings, the **Institutes** and **Conferences**. Regardless of how little we know about the external events of Cassian's life, these writings make him important to us, for they are the foundation of what we now call "western monasticism." They also give historical clues of the locations of various monasteries in Egypt. Cassian, in short, was the link between the east and west, and though not officially canonized, he is recognized as a saint in the eastern Church.

Scholars have debated over the years on the value of the **Institutes** and **Conferences** as historical sources for information on Egyptian monasticism or even whether they were written by Cassian. The conclusion most come to is that the writings are written in a conventional style and, therefore, are not authentic in the sense that the dialogues they contain actually took place. Nevertheless, they do represent the moral and ascetic ideals practiced by the Egyptian monks. Since the latter were hermits in contrast to cenobites, the eremitical life is stressed, though in Conference 19 he describes the two life-styles in such a way that neither is seen as superior to the other; both have their values. Two generations later, the eremitical ideal is still recognized—though not recommended for most monks—in the Rule of St. Benedict, which, for the most part, emphasizes life lived in community. Even today scholars debate about the degree of influence Cassian had on the Rule of Benedict, though none deny that he did indeed have an influence.

Quite simply, the **Institutes** deal largely with external practices observed by the monks of the desert while the **Conferences**
deal with interior practices of the heart and the spiritual life as
such. The **Institutes**, divided into twelve "books," describe such
external things as the following: clothing (clean, economical,
adapted to the area and climate of a region, providing for the
wants of the body with as little "fuss and entanglement" as possible); the way the Liturgy of the Hours is to be said (detailed even
to certain prayer postures, some of which still remain in vogue
today); the division of the hours of prayer (giving such common
sense considerations as, for example, requiring Sunday liturgies
to be celebrated with more solemnity and festivity so that a little
variety would increase devotion); and, finally, practical regulations and ascetic practices carried out within the monastery.
Each of these subjects comprises a "book," followed by a book
each on the principal faults monks must struggle against: gluttony, fornication, covetousness, anger, dejection, *accidie* (weari-
ness caused by the "noonday devil"), vainglory and pride. These
vices are easily recognizable as coming from those first spelled
out by Evagrius.

The **Conferences** deal with a number of topics pertaining to
the interior life: the meaning of monastic life, discretion (or
"discernment of spirits"), the three renunciations, the powers
that incite us to evil and, finally, the more positive aspects of
monastic life (prayer, chastity, spiritual knowledge, charisms and
so on). According to Cassian, the chief work of the monk is to
seek the kingdom of God. It is achieved through purity of heart,
about which he says:

> **It is to gain this that we should embrace solitude, suffer**
> **fastings, vigils, work, nakedness, devote ourselves to**
> **reading and to the practice of the other virtues, having**
> **no other purpose through all these things, than to make**
> **and to keep our heart invulnerable to all wicked passions**
> **and to mount, as by so many degrees, even to the perfec-**
> **tion of charity (Conf. 1,7).**

Purity of heart, in Cassian's terminology, is none other than the *apatheia* (liberation from disordered affections) proposed by Evagrius. Unlike the latter, however, Cassian leaves no doubt in the reader's mind that if purity of heart is a means in the spiritual life, love, not knowledge, is its end.

He sees the monastic life progress in three stages of renunciation, each leading to the next: the renunciation required when asceticism is practiced, the renunciation of sin and, finally, the renunciation of all that is not good. These deprivations would help lead the monks to humility and patience in ridding themselves of bad habits and passions. Patience would lead to peace or tranquility which achieved charity—a love which tended, eventually, to the perfection of the Father. However, as already pointed out, Cassian was realist enough to know there was no lasting renunciation unless there was a here and now corresponding compensation. Thus, restraint in one area meant to make room for spiritual joys; good tendencies had to replace those which needed to be cut off. For him, contemplation was the fruit of all renunciation; but it also enlivened and nourished the monk along the way.

It is when John Cassian speaks of prayer, however, that he reaches the heights of his doctrine. It can be summed up in St. Paul's phrase, "Pray always." Cassian claimed that "The aim of every monk and the perfection of his heart tends to continual and unbroken perseverance in prayer...(**Conf.** 9,2). For him, distractions at prayer were caused by distractions before prayer: "...therefore if we do not want anything to haunt us while we are praying, we should be careful before our prayer, to exclude it from the shrine of our heart" (ibid.). In order to help the monk attain this life of unceasing prayer, he recommended the repetition of a short formula: "Oh God, make speed to save me; Oh Lord, make haste to help me" (**Conf.** 2,10). It is not unlike the practice of using a "mantra" suggested to those who like eastern forms of meditation today.

Many more choice sayings from this master of the monastic life could be cited. Some of them, dealing with the monk's conduct in choir, are amusing to modern readers. However, in closing, it may be more profitable to quote one sentence from his **Conferences** which sums up his entire teaching: "This, I say, is the end of all perfection, that the mind, purged from all carnal desires may daily be lifted toward spiritual things, until the whole life and all the thoughts of the heart become one continuous prayer" (2,7).

BENEDICT OF NURSIA

Master of Moderation

Like a mighty oak, the tree of Benedictinism, as we know it today, started from a little acorn; we might say a "reluctant acorn." Many years ago, the English author, Aldous Huxley, in the context of attesting to the tree's flourishing growth, wrote: "Europe owes an incalculable debt to the young man, who, because he was more interested in knowing God than in getting on, or even 'doing good' in the world, left Rome for that burrow in the hillside above Subiaco." Yes, St. Benedict was a dropout. According to his biographer, Pope St. Gregory the Great, he was a small town boy, born in 480 A.D., in Nursia (now Norcia), Italy, about seventy miles northeast of Rome.

The spirit animating the saint who authored the Benedictine Rule is certainly authentically recorded in the second book of **Dialogues**, even though Gregory, himself a follower of Benedict during the next century, tends to idealize his spiritual father. His recording of Benedict's life—the only one we have available—despite its hyperbole and acknowledged historical difficulties, makes interesting reading. Further, today many of the events in the account have been verified by other less biased fifth century eyewitnesses. Basically, the story runs as follows.

Sent to Rome by his parents to obtain a liberal education, Benedict soon feared that he, like many of his fellow students, would be drawn into a life of sin. Attributing the downfall of his

161

BENEDICT

WORK

PRAY

friends to the learning they were receiving, he "...turned his back on further studies, gave up home and inheritance and resolved to embrace the religious life. He took this step, well aware of his ignorance, yet wise, uneducated though he was" (**Dialogues**, Book II, Ch. 1).

After his departure, one of the many miraculous happenings, sprinkled generously throughout the account, was the instantaneous mending, through Benedict's prayers, of a broken tray borrowed by his beloved nurse, the sole companion of his journey. The notoriety resulting from this event caused him to leave his nurse secretly and to make his way alone to Subiaco, thirty-five miles from Rome. Along the way, he met a monk, Romanus, who, discovering the young man's purpose, clothed him in the monastic habit and helped him pursue his goal. For three years, unknown to anyone but Romanus, Benedict remained hidden in a narrow cave, having his needs supplied by this monk. The latter, according to the account, saved a portion of his own daily food allowance and, since there was no path leading to the cave, lowered it to Benedict's hideaway by means of a rope. The recluse was alerted to the approach of his meal by means of a little bell attached to the rope.

Eventually the hermit was discovered, first by a priest, then by some shepherds, and finally by some monks of a nearby monastery who asked him to be their superior, their own abbot having recently died. It was only by dint of heavy persuasion that Benedict gave in to their wish for, in his heart, he knew his standards of monastic discipline would not be to their liking. Time proved him correct in this assessment. Like most of us, "They could not see why they should have to force their settled minds into new ways of thinking" (II, 3). To solve their problem, they resolved to poison the new abbot's wine. During the meal, however, Benedict made his customary sign of the cross over the deadly drink, instantaneously shattering the cup to pieces "...as if he had struck it with a stone" (ibid.). In equivalent terms, he calmly told the monks, "I told you so," and suggested they find an abbot more to their liking.

He left them and returned to his desert retreat. His influence,

however, soon began to be felt again in the surrounding coun-
tryside and "...because of his signs and wonders, a great number
of men gathered around him to devote themselves to God's service. Christ blessed his work and before long he had established
twelve monasteries with an abbot and twelve monks in each of
them. There were a few other monks whom he kept with him,
since he felt that they still needed his personal guidance" (II, 4).
With these words of Gregory we begin to see the tree of this
reluctant student, reluctant abbot, becoming what today represents the oak of a worldwide network of persons devoted to
seeking God according to a life-style patterned on his. To mention only a few who converted or influenced whole nations during the history of the Church we have Boniface of Germany,
Augustine of Canterbury, Bede the Venerable, also of England,
and Ansgar of Denmark.

The **Dialogues** continue, stylistically, to give extravagant
accounts of the saint's miraculous powers: causing springs to
flow in dry places; causing an iron blade to rise from the bottom
of a lake and to re-attach itself to its handle; the saving from
drowning of a young monk, Placid, through the obedience of
another monk, Maurus, who, at Benedict's word, walked on the
waters of the lake, and so on. Another feat concerned the protection of the saint by a raven which intercepted and disposed of
a piece of poisoned bread given to Benedict by a priest jealous
of the former's reputation. Later, we are told, the priest was
crushed to death when the balcony on which he stood collapsed.
To the surprise of his monks, this accident and death of his
enemy caused much sorrow in the heart of their abbot. It was
after this incident that Benedict left Subiaco, soon afterward to
found the famed Abbey of Monte Cassino.

Even Gregory concedes the amazing quality of these miracles
and, to get his point across, he makes the following comparisons
with great biblical personages: "The water streaming from the
rock reminds me of Moses, and the iron blade that rose from
the bottom of the lake, Eliseus. The walking on the water recalls
St. Peter, the obedience of the raven, Elias, and the grief at the
death of an enemy, David" (II, 8). Other miracles include several

against evil powers; multiplying grain and oil in time of famine; the curing of a leper; the raising of two boys to life; and events which today we might call "parapsychological phenomena," such as reading hearts and prophetic messages. Some of the prophecies Gregory attributes to Benedict include the number of years Totila the Goth would rule and when he would die, the destruction of Rome by storms and earthquakes, and the first destruction of Monte Cassino (by Lombards) which took place sometime between 580-589 A.D. At the conclusion of the second book, Gregory reports that Benedict foresaw his own death, also, giving orders for his tomb to be opened six days prior to it.

After waxing eloquently on the virtues of Benedict, Gregory culminates everything by concluding that he possessed "the spirit of all the just." Yet even this loyal son of Benedict admitted there was one time the man of God was unable to have a wish fulfilled. In a delightful story concerning an annual visit to his sister, Scholastica pleads with him to remain longer than usual so they could "'keep on talking about the joys of heaven'" (II, 33). Benedict, surprised that she would ask him to violate the monastic rule of enclosure, told her so. But she, in response to his refusal, folded her hands and bowed her head in prayer. Suddenly a burst of lightning and thunder caused such a downpour that Benedict and his companions were unable to leave. To his consternation and protestations, Scholastica replied, "'When I appealed to you, you would not listen to me. So I turned to my God and he heard my prayer. Leave now if you can. Leave me here and go back to your monastery'" (ibid.) Gregory comments, a bit chauvinistically, that Benedict's wish "...was thwarted by a miracle God performed in answer to a woman's prayer," though he adds, surprisingly, "...it is no more than right that her influence was greater than his, since hers was the greater love" (ibid.). Nevertheless, Benedict loved greatly too. There seems to be evidence that he enjoyed some kind of a mystical experience before his death in which he saw the whole world gathered up before him in what appeared to be a single ray of light.

Whether Gregory's account is over-dramatized or not, there is no denying the dramatic impact Benedict's followers have had on human history. As Aldous Huxley's remark at the beginning of this article indicates, they were the preservers of European culture during medieval times. In the context, he cites a few of the contributions: sharing their worship and their experience of God with those who lived in the same region; attacking thorny social questions, especially by combating economic evils through a revival of agriculture and the draining of swamps; and fighting the evils of ignorance through various kinds of education. Huxley is careful to note, however, that these works were always accomplished at the margins of society rather than at its center. The well-known motto, "prayer and work" kept Benedictines from thrusting themselves headlong into activity for activity's sake.

The Rule of Benedict itself is the most authentic source we have of his personality. It has often been praised, in comparison to the more ascetical rules of the east, for its discretion. In it, Benedict made adaptations which resulted from a combination of all he had learned of monasticism from the fathers of the east and his own knowledge of the monks in the west. A rather amusing example of this can be found in Chapter 40: "Although we read that wine is not at all proper for monks, yet, because monks in our times cannot be persuaded of this, let us agree to this at least, that we do not drink to satiety, but sparingly; because 'wine maketh even wise men fall off.'"

Basically, the life legislated for in the Rule is Christo-centric: "May nothing be preferred to the love of Christ" (Ch. 4) and sacramental: the cellarer is to "...look upon all the utensils of the monastery and its whole property as upon the sacred vessels of the altar" (Ch. 31). The role of abbot is unique in Benedict's monasteries. As model, the abbot is to enflesh the Rule daily through word and deed (Ch. 2); as center of unity he is to "accommodate himself to all in such a way that he may not only suffer no loss in the sheep committed to him but may even rejoice in the increase of a good flock" (ibid.); as collaborator with his monks, he is to call the whole community together for counsel in important matters so as to discern God's will for them in the concrete world in which they live. Even the youngest monks are to be called for counsel because "God often reveals what is better to the younger" (Ch. 3).

Detailed prescriptions are spelled out in the Rule for the daily monastic routine, yet these specifics are tempered by the discretion and moderation for which Benedict is famous. Modifications and concessions are made throughout for those who may have been excommunicated from community functions for faults (Ch. 27), for the sick (Ch. 36), for the young and old (Ch. 37), for the weekly reader (Ch. 38), for the kind of clothing to be worn in different climates (Ch. 55), for pilgrim monks (Ch. 61), for those who go on a journey (Ch. 67), and so on. Three virtues singled out in the Rule as having special importance for Benedictines are obedience, silence, and humility (Chs. 5, 6, 7). Historically, they have built up a reputation for emphasizing two other "virtues" proposed by their founder as well: the pursuit of peace (Prologue: "...seek peace and pursue it") and hospitality (Ch. 53: "Let all guests that come be received like Christ"). Monasteries, in the Rule, are not founded for particular works; instead, of all the works monks might do, "nothing is to be preferred to the Work of God" (Ch. 43), that is, the liturgy, where work and prayer, joined together, become THE work of God.

Is it any wonder that in 1858 John Henry Cardinal Newman wrote a commentary praising St. Benedict's followers for the slow but sure social revolution they effected during the barbarian invasions; or that, in 1947, Pope Pius XII wrote an encyclical, "Like a Star," which honored the fourteenth centenary of the saint's death; or that Pope Paul VI, in 1964, when consecrating the abbey church of Monte Cassino, rebuilt once more after allied bombers had destroyed it during World War II, proclaimed Benedict "Patron and Protector of Europe"? We think not.

Raise up in your Church, O Lord, the spirit with which our holy Father Benedict was animated, that filled with the same spirit, we may study to love what he loved and to practice what he taught.

RADEGUND

Queen of the Franks

St. Radegund would have resonated with the kind of environment portrayed in the PBS series, "I, Claudius." She, too, lived in a situation of crisis and was frequently confronted with violence, murder and intrigue. A native of Thuringia (in Germany), she was one of the first Frankish women to establish and have significant influence over the monasteries in France. Most of the biographical information we have about Radegund is found in the writings of her friend Venantius Fortunatus and Baudonivia, one of her former pupils and a nun in her monastery. The biographies they wrote and other sketchier accounts differ in the details of her life but they all follow a similar pattern as to general content.

When the king of Thuringia died in the early sixth century, the land was divided between his three sons. Hermanfried, the most powerful, goaded on by his wife (daughter of Theodoric, the famous Ostrogothic king of Italy), assassinated his brother Berthaire, who was Radegund's father. They also connived to eliminate the other brother, Balderic, so that Hermanfried could become the sole ruler. In order to accomplish this wicked scheme Hermanfried entered into an alliance with Thierry, eldest son of Clovis, king of the Franks. This was a definite switch because the Thuringians and Franks had been enemies for years. Further, Radegund's unscrupulous uncle had, in the past, broken a treaty with the Franks, murdering a number of their women and children.

Thierry, angered when Hermanfried overreached himself in the territory agreed upon as the price of his cooperation, asked his brother Clothar for assistance. The Franks, enraged, took revenge by invading Thuringia in 531 A.D., devastating the country and carrying off valuable booty and prisoners of war. They almost obliterated the ruling house. The traumatic experience of this encounter has been preserved in a poem, "The Thuringian War," written thirty years later, either by Radegund or her friend Fortunatus, with her collaboration. Here are some excerpts from the poem, written to her cousin Amalfred who escaped the tribal war:

> **Alas, the corpses lie shamefully unburied on the field,**
>> **An entire people, strewn in a common grave.**
> **Not Troy alone must mourn her ruins:**
>> **The Thuringian land suffered equal slaughter...**
> **A wife's naked feet trod in her husband's blood**
>> **And the tender sister stepped over the fallen brother.**
> **The boy torn from his mother's embrace, his funeral plaint**
>> **Hung on her lips, with all her tears unshed...**
> **Oh Amalfred, remember how it was in those first years,**
>> **How I was your own Radegund then.**
> **An infant, how you cherished me then.**
>> **Son of my father's brother, kindly kinsman**
> **(quoted in Sainted Women of the Dark Ages, edited and**
>> **translated by Jo Ann McNamara and John E. Halborg**
>> **with E. Gordon Whatley, Duke University Press, 1992,**
>> **pp. 66-68).**

As a reward for his part in the war, Clothar was awarded the orphaned children of Berthaire, Radegund and her younger brother. Clothar was the son of St. Clothild but in no way did he resemble his mother. On the contrary, he married his brother Clodomir's widow and murdered her sons. The little princess Radegund had much in common with Clothild for she had spent her first years in the house of an uncle who had murdered her father. Intended by Clothar to be his future queen, she was sent to his country home in Athies in order to be educated. At a very young age, Radegund showed a definite learning toward things spiritual. Fortunatus tells us:

> **While but a small child...she would also carry out what she had planned beforehand with Samuel, a little cleric. Following his lead, carrying a wooden cross they had made, singing psalms, the children would troop into the oratory as somber as adults (ibid., p. 71).**

In Athies the horrors through which she had lived up until now began to diminish. Her teachers were competent and she progressed well in her studies, especially in a study of the Gospel which soon fascinated her. The day of her baptism was her initiation into vigorous efforts to imitate Christ closely, even to death if possible. Fortunatus notes, "The maiden was taught letters and other things suitable to her sex and she would often converse with other children there about her desire to be a martyr if the chance came in her time" (ibid., p. 71).

When she was nineteen she was sent for by Clothar and compelled to become his queen. He had several wives and it was said she was the fifth of seven. He was unbearable, and since she was unable to please him, she turned her attention to prayer, austerities and serving the poor. In fact, she was so devoted to charitable works that she often kept him waiting at meals. At night she left him frequently under any pretext. Fortunatus summarizes the situation:

> **...though married to a terrestrial prince, she was not separated from the celestial one and, the more secular power was bestowed upon her, the more humbly she bent her will—more than befitted her royal status. Always subject to God following priestly admonitions, she was more Christ's partner than her husband's companion (ibid., p. 72).**

In a passage highly charged with eucharistic overtones, he also praises her work for the unfortunate: "With that holy woman, acts of mercy were no fewer than the crowds who pressed her;

as there was no shortage of those who asked, so was there no shortage in what she gave so that, wonderfully, they could all be satisfied" (ibid., p. 77). In addition to serving the poor, she used her influence as a woman and queen to become an advocate for other causes, which today we would call "social justice issues." Fortunatus gives an example:

> ...if the king, according to custom, condemned a guilty criminal to death, wasn't the most holy queen near dead with torment lest the culprit perish by the sword? How she would rush about among his trusty men, ministers and nobles, whose blandishments might soothe the prince's temper until the king's anger ceased and the voice of salvation flowed where the sentence of death had issued before (ibid., p. 74).

Quarrels were frequent between Radegund and her husband. He was violent and he often complained she had turned his court into a cloister. The final blow came when he killed her brother. (One account said he also murdered one of his own sons together with his wife and children by burning them alive in their home.) After six years of his abuse, Radegund left the life of the court. Fortunatus records that she asked Bishop Medard to clothe her in the habit of a nun and consecrate her to God. When he hesitated because he was afraid of incurring the king's wrath, she entered the sacristy, put on a monastic garb and went up to the altar, saying to him: "If you refuse to consecrate me, a lamb will be lost to the flock" (quoted in **Woman Under Monasticism** by Lina Eckenstein, Cambridge: At The University Press, 1896, p. 54). The bishop was so shocked he laid his hand on her and consecrated her as a deaconess. The editors of **Sainted Women of the Dark Ages** (op. cit., p. 75) comment that this seems to be the bishop's ingenious solution to the sticky problem of consecrating a woman still married to a king. Deaconesses were not bound by celibacy!

The information we have surrounding Radegund's leaving the king are conflictual. One account (**Lives of Sainted Queens**, no author given, London: Burns and Oates; New York: Benziger Brothers, no date, p. 5) claims Clothar was happy to get rid of her at first but later was sorry he had let her go and went to reclaim her. This might explain the account which says she settled temporarily in a villa between Tours and Poitiers, which he had provided, but that she left when she found out he was coming. She then went to Poitiers where she founded a monastery. Others, namely Fortunatus, emphasize the daring of her escape, while she herself emphasizes Clothar's generosity in supporting her religious life until death. We can only conclude that he did try to reclaim her at some point, but that eventually they came to some kind of amicable arrangement by which he, resigned to his loss, allowed her to pursue her chosen vocation. Eckenstein (op. cit., p. 55) claims that after this Radegund, in letters to bishops, referred to Clothar as "the noble Lord" and not as her husband.

It is believed he was in Tours in 558 A.D. seeking absolution for his sinful life, and when it became evident he would soon die he tried to make amends by richly endowing the monastery in Poitiers. At the time of his death in 561 he was sole ruler over the kingdom, which included France, Burgundy, Thuringia, and even parts of Italy and Spain. After he died, Radegund settled in Poitiers permanently and the Council of Tours (566) formally put her monastery under its protection. It is implied by Fortunatus and Baudonivia that she lived a quiet and serene life after Clothar's death, but history tells a different story. Eckenstein notes that the land was divided between his four sons and that, afterward, "plots, counterplots and unceasing warfare" (op. cit., p. 56) ensued for forty years. We are not told how Radegund reacted to any of this intrigue and violence. However, Baudonivia says she wrote frequently to her royal friends trying to secure peace, and that she had her nuns praying for this intention unceasingly.

The monastery of Poitiers was named "Holy Cross" in honor of the relic of the true Cross, sent by Emperor Justin at Radegund's request. Baudonivia records an interesting incident in this regard which gives us insight into the personality of Radegund. It seems she was capable of a little intrigue herself!

The story reveals that King Sigebert had given Radegund permission to request the relic from the emperor, but the local bishop (who was hostile toward her) would not permit it to be received by the people. Baudonivia remarks that, "her spirit blazing in a fighting mood, she sent again to the benevolent king to say that they did not wish to receive Salvation itself into the city!" (McNamara and others, op. cit., p. 98). Then she took the relic of the Cross, brought it to a male monastery which the king had founded in Tours and began fasting and doing penance until the bishop relented. Venantius Fortunatus, afterward the bishop of Poitiers, composed two hymns for the occasion of the installation of the prized relic—*Vexilla regis prodeunt* (The royal banners forward go) and *Pange lingua gloriosi* (Praise to Christ's immortal body)—which are still used in our liturgy.

It is difficult to sort out the "real" Radegund if we read the information supplied by the two who should have known her best. Both of her biographers emphasize the fact that she despoiled herself of her royal apparel and jewels because, at that time, it was characteristic of Frankish royalty to love sumptuous clothing. Both of them claim, also, that she never asked anyone to do anything she herself had not done, but after these comments, the accounts part company. Fortunatus glorifies her as an ascetic, one in a long line of heroic martyrs, while Baudonivia glorifies her as a miracle-worker. Fortunatus, for example, says this "queen by birth and marriage, mistress of the palace, served the poor as a handmaid," and, "...from the time she was veiled, consecrated by St. Medard, even in illness, she ate nothing but legumes and green vegetables: not fruit nor fish nor eggs" (ibid., pp. 72, 76). He said that if she were praised when she wore a new veil, she would take it off and send it to the nearest church to be used as an altar cloth. She also fed paupers twice a week and bathed them. Then "...if she noticed that anyone's clothes were shoddy with age, she would take them away and give them new ones. Thus she spruced up all who came to the feast in rags" (ibid., p. 77).

Fortunatus also quotes an attendant who noticed Radegund kissing a leper, saying, "'Most holy lady, when you have embraced lepers, who will kiss you?' Pleasantly, she answered: 'Really, if you won't kiss me, it's no concern of mine'" (ibid., p. 78). Finally, he recounts numerous personal austerities that Radegund practiced. It is questionable, however, as to how many of these are authentic as Gregory of Tours does not mention any extreme practices in his account. At the end of his biography, Fortunatus tells about the many miraculous cures worked by Radegund both before and after her death. In fact, he is so caught up in his recital that he neglects to say anything about how she spent the last days of her life. Though he seems overly zealous in making a martyr out of her, his poetry paints quite another picture. He portrays the nuns at Poitiers living in an idyllic setting of loving and intimate sharing of learning and poetry. This depiction is not altogether true, either, as the wars which took place after Clothar's death had serious consequences for her monastery. Some involved in the conflicts were her relatives by marriage and some of them eventually entered the community.

Baudonivia's biography does not have a title. Instead, her introduction addresses all of "Holy Radegund's congregation." She is very effusive and wordy as we can see in this passage: "Who can describe her patience, charity, fervor of spirit, prudence, beneficence, holy zeal, and incessant 'meditating on the law of God by day and by night'" (ibid., p. 91). In praise of her mentor, Baudonivia introduces an amusing incident: "The praise of God was so ever-present to her heart and tongue that once when she saw Eodegund the portress crossing the yard and wished to call her, she shouted, 'Alleluia,' instead of her name. She did that a thousand times but she never uttered any slander or lies, or curses against anyone" (ibid.). Though extravagant in extolling Radegund, it must be admitted Baudonivia does insert a personal touch into her narrative. She quotes the former queen saying to her nuns, "Daughters, I chose you. You are my light and my life. You are my rest and all my happiness, my new plantation" (ibid.).

She also notes the details of community life at Poitiers and indicates that Radegund, a good listener, tried to teach her nuns to be good listeners too: "She ordained that a lesson would always be read while we were eating, so that we would not only

receive food for the jaws but the Word of God for the ears"
(ibid., p. 100). Finally, one of the many miracles Baudonivia
credits her heroine with concerns a raucous night bird who was
breaking the silence of the monastery. When one of the nuns
asked if Radegund would allow her to use her name to get rid of
it, the saint told her, "If it troubles you, go and make the sign of
the cross over it in the Lord's name." The nun "walked over and
said to the bird: 'In the name of our Lord Jesus Christ, Lady
Radegund orders you to leave this place unless you came at
God's behest and presume to sing no more within it.'" Her biographer adds with pride, "Then, as if the creature had heard the
words from God's own mouth, it took flight and was never seen
again. She had earned the obedience of birds and beasts, for she
had never failed to obey the Lord's commands" (ibid.).

Though it is quite accurate to say that Radegund founded the
monastery at Poitiers and that she was its greatest influence, she
appointed another woman, Agnes, as the abbess. Some think this
was a gesture of humility; others say it was because she considered Agnes' virginal state superior to her own. Before Radegund
died, she made a trip to Arles to become more familiar with
Caesarius' Rule, which she had adopted for the nuns, so as to better instruct them. Baudonivia reported that before the saint's
death she also had a vision of the Lord who appeared to her as a
young man. He said to her,

**"Why then have you sought me, with burning desire, with
so many tears? Why do you plead, groaning, and call out
in copious prayer, afflicting such agony upon yourself for
my sake who am always by your side? Oh, my precious
gem, you must know that you are the first jewel in the
crown on my head" (ibid., p. 101).**

One account says she received the last sacraments with the nuns
surrounding her bed, promising them she would be with them
always; then she died while praising God. Baudonivia is very
explicit in saying the day was Christmas "since she had always
chosen to do the things she cared most about on the birthday of

the Lord" (ibid., p. 101). The authors quoting her (op. cit.), however, clarify by saying there was a tradition that Jesus was born on a Wednesday, the day of the creation of the sun and moon, and that her actual death date was August 13, 587 A.D. One author says the bishop of Poitiers was absent at the time, so the nuns invited Gregory of Tours to bury her. Others note that the "absent" bishop was the same one who was hostile toward her. Whatever the circumstances, no doubt she had a splendid funeral with her friend officiating. As a matter of fact, Gregory wrote a detailed description of it, saying some two hundred women crowded around the bier crying,

> **To whom, mother, have you left us orphans? To whom shall we turn in our distress? We left our parents, our relatives and our homes, and we followed you. What have we before us now, but tears unceasing, and grief that can never end? Truly, this monastery is to us more than the greatness of village and city.... The earth is now darkened to us, this place has been straitened since we no longer behold your countenance. Woe to us who are left by our holy mother! Happy those who left this world while you were still alive... (quoted in Eckenstein, op. cit., p. 65).**

The incessant fighting taking place outside the monastery invaded it after the deaths of Radegund and, later, Abbess Agnes. One of the daughters of the warring parties had been sent to the monastery while Radegund was still living, and after her death she led dissident forces that eventually tore it apart. In 1562 the French Calvinists violated Radegund's tomb, but, though Poitiers was burned and looted during the wars, her monastery still exists today and the people of Poitiers venerate her as their patroness.

GREGORY
THE GREAT

The Watchman

We who live in a nuclear age and face the possibility of seeing the destruction of our planet can rightly attest that ours is the most dangerous time in the history of the human race. People of other ages have made the same claim. When Pope St. Gregory the Great lived, so alarming was the situation following the defeat of the Goths and Vandals in Italy, that he was convinced, as he described in one of his letters, the end times had come. The invasion by the Lombards was imminent and the Tiber had overflowed its banks, leaving in its path destruction of property and crops with the danger of famine and disease to follow.

There is no record of the date of Gregory's birth. Some guess at 540 A.D., about ten years after St. Benedict of Nursia founded his monastic group. Well born, his father being wealthy and holding an office of senatorial rank with the title, *Regionarius*, Gregory received a good education and was said to have been an apt student. Gregory of Tours, who was an historian of this time, said he was the most knowledgeable person in Rome in the areas of grammar, rhetoric and logic. It seems he also studied law. He did not have what we call a "liberal education" however, for he studied little history and no languages other than his own, the study of Greek literature and scientific culture having died out in Rome. Later, Gregory devoted himself strictly to the study of devotional works—Scripture and the Latin Fathers, especially St.

Augustine. Unlike many other Fathers of the Church, he condemned the study of classical literature. In his letter to
Desiderious we read:

> ....if, hereafter, what has been reported to us should
> prove evidently to be false, and it should be clear that
> you do not apply yourself to trifles and secular literature,
> we shall give thanks to our God, who has not permitted
> your heart to be stained with the blasphemous praises of
> the abominable (heathen); and we will treat without mis-
> giving or hesitation concerning the granting of what you
> request (Bk. 11, Letter 54).

His early education fitted him for taking care of practical as
well as religious matters and he was able to speak forcibly on
those with which he was acquainted. At first he pursued the
ordinary secular occupations of the day and was indistinguish-
able from others in regard to dress or behavior. Emperor Justin
II gave him the rank of *Praetor Urbanus* when Gregory was only
about thirty years of age. This political office promised a brilliant secular career. Though he had long wrestled with the desire
to follow Jesus through the evangelical counsels, it is clear he
was an ordinary person in every way—neither irreligious nor particularly religious at this time.

Nevertheless, he was brought up religiously by his father
Gordianus and his mother Silvia, who lived in seclusion as an
ascetic after her husband's death. His father's sisters Tarsilla and
Aemilian, who lived as virgins in their own home, are listed in
the calendar of the saints. Gregory admitted that he found it
hard to live for God in his early life though he never gave us any
clues about a particular crisis or an attachment to sin during his
youth. After his father's death his religious development became
more pronounced. He kept only a small part of the patrimony
he inherited and gave the rest to charitable causes, especially to
found six monasteries on the family estates, and a seventh in
which he himself lived as a monk.

He believed, as was the teaching of his day, that monastic life was the highest form of Christian living. This belief and his great admiration for St. Benedict of Nursia resulted in Gregory practicing the austerity of the Rule of St. Benedict to an extreme degree. His biographer said he ate only raw vegetables, supplied by his mother, and that his fasts constantly jeopardized not only his health but his life. In his **Dialogues** he admits that one year he fainted from exhaustion at the end of Holy Week. Rather than break his Lenten fast, he begged the prayers of a holy monk. His rigorous life-style, however, did not deter him from steadfast habits of study, prayer and physical work.

A favorite incident recorded by historians was the day he caught sight of some English youths in the Roman slave market. He was impelled to ask permission to go to England as a missionary to convert those who practiced this form of detestable slavery. Although Benedict I had given permission, he recalled Gregory at the insistence of the Roman people. Later, his dream of converting the English was realized when, as pope, he sent the one whom we now know as St. Augustine of Canterbury. Gregory, returning to Rome, spent a relatively short but happy time in his monastery. Then he was ordained deacon and sent to Constantinople to be regional deacon of the pope in the imperial court (574-578 A.D.).

It has not been recorded which pope ordained him priest, though some think it must have been the same Benedict I who had ordination in mind when sending him to Constantinople. In 579 Gregory was made ambassador to the court of Emperor Tiberius II, where his chief work was to stifle the Lombards, against whom the emperor proved very ineffective. Letters of Gregory from this period indicate that he had many influential friends in the court with whom he communicated long after his departure. Among many dignitaries were the emperor's sister and his physician, as well as Leander, Bishop of Seville, who happened to be living in Constantinople at the time. It was the latter who persuaded Gregory to write a book on morality, known to us as his **Commentary on the Book of Job**. Gregory was enabled to live outside his monastery and take up his secular court duties only because of these friends.

In 585 Gregory was recalled to Rome where the Lombards endangered not only Italy but the city itself. At this time he was elected abbot of his beloved monastery. He found the next five years the happiest of his life. Then Pope Pelagius II died of a disease rampant in the country and Gregory's peace was ended when the clergy and people of Rome elected him pope. Since the situation of the country had so deteriorated, he was unwilling to undertake the task. He fled the city in disguise but, when found, was persuaded to return and be their shepherd. His consecration took place on September 3, 590 A.D., the date still observed as his feast.

At the time of his election there was no separate emperor in the west and the eastern emperor lived in far off Constantinople. This historical situation combined with the aggressive activities of the Lombards accounts for Gregory assuming great importance as a political leader. This is evident in his letters which include complaints about the corruption and abuses found in the civil officers of the west. Today these letters make for interesting reflection in light of current debates about how much the clergy should get involved in politics. Gregory, a good ruler, tells us how he viewed his role in the Church in his own words:

"I have made you a watchman for the house of Israel." ...A watchman always stands on a height so that he can see from afar what is coming. ...Since I assumed the burden of pastoral care, my mind can no longer be collected; it is concerned with so many matters. I am forced to consider the affairs of the Church and of the monasteries. ...I am responsible for the concerns of our citizens. I must worry about the invasions of roving bands of barbarians, and beware of the wolves who lie in wait for my flock. ...So who am I to be a watchman, for I do not stand on the mountain of action but lie down in the valley of weakness? Truly the all-powerful Creator and Redeemer can give me in spite of my weaknesses a higher life and effective speech... (Homily I on Ezechiel 40:1-48).

WRITINGS OF GREGORY

During his reign Gregory's numerous letters were compiled into fourteen books, each representing a year of his pontificate. They range on every subject from political concerns to those of liturgical execution. They give us insights into the times in which he lived and into his personality, especially in regard to his personal concern even for the Lombards. In one letter, to their queen, Theodelinda, a Catholic, written shortly before his death, he congratulates her for having her son baptized and sent, as gift, a portion of what was reputedly from the true cross. In addition to these letters, we have twenty-two homilies on Ezechiel and forty on the Gospels. His work on morality, already mentioned, was probably the first manual we have on moral and ascetical theology. Consider how we have been schooled to think in the following way:

You must know that sin can be committed in three ways. It is done either in ignorance, in weakness, or of set purpose. And certainly the sin committed in weakness is more grave than that done in ignorance; but that done of set purpose is much more grave than that done in weakness (Commentary on the Book of Job, Bk. 25, 11, 18).

In his book, **Pastoral Care**, we find just that—Gregory's care for the churches under his jurisdiction, and his views on the role of a bishop. He sees him as ruler, spiritual guide, preacher, teacher, spiritual physician and as intercessor before God for his people.

His best known work, the **Dialogue**s, includes a section on the life of St. Benedict. Because it is obviously the narration of one who saw Benedict as his hero it cannot be relied on for absolute historical accuracy. Nevertheless, it does give us a good picture, in broad outline, of the founder of western monasticism as well as insights into its author. Gregory was, first of all, a monk and we find in his writings the earliest interpretation of what the relationship should be between bishops and the monastics in their dioceses. This pattern has not varied too much over the centuries. We also find, because of his particular monastic orientation, the beginning of a teaching on celibacy for the clergy.

Gregory was one of two popes in history titled, "the great" (the other was Leo I), though he saw himself as a "servant of the servants of God"—a title which originated with him and is still used by popes today. Truly a watchman for his people, he was "great" in the history of the Church. He laid the foundations for the medieval papacy that governed the western world after the fall of the western empire in the sixth century. He died on March 12, 604 A.D., actively corresponding with the churches right up to the end.

HROSWITHA

Playwright and Poet

The first known dramatist of Christianity, the first Saxon poet and the earliest known historian of Germany was a canoness who lived in the Benedictine monastery of Gandersheim in Saxony. However, all the information we have on the life of Hroswitha comes from what we can surmise about the times in which she lived and from the conjectures we can make when reading her writings, none of which are "autobiographical" in the usual sense of the word. This is unfortunate indeed, because her writings reveal to us a very astute and clever woman.

What, then, do we know? Though the tenth century was known as the "Dark Ages," Germany enjoyed more enlightened learning than most other countries due to the renaissance of the Carolingian Empire. At the end of the ninth century there were twenty monasteries in Saxony. Of these, eleven were "nunneries" as they were called at the time. They housed both vowed nuns and canonesses. One of the monasteries was Gandersheim, which was consecrated on All Saints' Day in 881. It was founded by Duke Liudolf at the request of his Frankish wife, Oda, and her mother, Aeda, who had seen a vision of St. John the Baptist which informed her that her famous son-in-law would establish a cloister for saintly women. It is in Hroswitha's writings that we learn that Liudolf had been in the service of Louis I, grandson of Charlemagne and King of the Franks.

Liudolf and Oda made a pilgrimage to Rome to obtain relics for the monastery and to receive the blessing of Pope Sergius II, having petitioned King Louis I for an introduction to the pope.

Impressed, the latter gave them the bones "of two mighty shep-herds, Anastasius, the most holy bishop of his throne, and his co-apostle, the sacred Innocent" (recorded by Hroswitha in her **Primordia**). The relics were carried off to Saxony and Anastasius and Innocent became the patron saints of Gandersheim. It became the most distinguished of all the monasteries founded by Liudolf, whose descendants ruled Germany during Hroswitha's time. Because it was quite common for members of the families of patrons to enter these monasteries, it is not surprising to find that the first three abbesses of Gandersheim were daughters of Liudolf and Oda.

In 959 Princess Gerberga II became the Abbess. It has been deduced that Hroswitha was born about 935 A.D., because one time she wrote that her Abbess, the Princess Gerberga, whose known date of birth was 940, was younger than she. The exact date of Hroswitha's death is also unknown but historians have suggested sometime between 1001-1002. Her teacher and friend, Gerberga II, was the daughter of Henry, Duke of Bavaria and niece of Otto I, Henry's brother. During his reign, Otto I con-quered northern Italy and was crowned King of the Lombards. Because he restored law and order in Italy, Pope John XII hon-ored him with the Imperial Crown and thus he became the founder of the Holy Roman Empire of the German people.

Otto I, a born statesman, also encouraged and sponsored learning. Hroswitha wrote a history of his reign, **Gesta Ottonis**, which was memorialized in a 1501 publication of her works. In it is a picture executed by the famous artist, Albrecht Dürer, which shows her kneeling before the Emperor, presenting her book to him with the Abbess Gerberga looking on. It is conjec-tured that Hroswitha entered the monastery in 955, the year in which Otto II was born. Later, he ruled with his father as co-emperor of the Holy Roman Empire. He also became a good friend of our poet.

These historical connections all serve to point up the kind of environment in which Hroswitha lived—one that encouraged the pursuit of learning, art and poetry. She recounts that she often came into contact with scholars as well as ecclesiastical personages and members of the royalty, all closely associated with one another. Abbess Gerberga and her sister learned Greek and so it was quite possible Hroswitha learned the language too. She does use Greek sources in some of her stories.

Gandersheim was considered a "free" abbey, which meant that the abbess was directly responsible to the king rather than to the church. However, in 947, Otto I freed the abbey from royal rule and gave the abbess supreme authority. She had her own court of law, sent soldiers to battle, coined her own money and had a right to a seat in the Imperial Diet. Under her jurisdiction were the nuns and canonesses of the abbey. (Current expressions of feminism seem less radical when we discover how much power some women exercised in the early days of the Church!) The "canonesses," whose title appears for the first time in the eighth century, vowed chastity and obedience but not the vow of poverty as professed by the nuns. Their life-style was less strict too. They were allowed to receive guests, to go in and out of the monastery with permission, and to own books and property. They were also allowed to have servants. They did, however, following the Rule of St. Benedict, live a communal life and participated fully in the daily recitation of the Divine Office.

We know nothing of Hroswitha's background, but we can infer that she was of noble birth, because only novices from noble families were chosen for entrance into the monasteries of her time. Her name has been spelled in many ways but she called herself *Clamor Validus Gandersheimensis*, the "strong voice of Gandersheim." The reason some give for the fact that her name and works were not known for so many centuries is that before the twelfth century it was not the custom to record the names of anyone who was not clearly a Church dignitary or of the royalty. So even though Hroswitha was very scholarly and made her monastery famous, she was considered just a lowly canoness.

It is believed she entered the abbey at a very young age. Her skill in Latin indicates she had many years of training from teachers very well versed in the language. Hroswitha's knowledge of classical and religious literature give evidence that Gandersheim must have had a rich collection of manuscripts and an excellent library. Indeed, she said she obtained all her information from the monastic library. Some scholars believe, because of the influence seen in her writings, that she was acquainted with, among other writings, Virgil's **Aeneid**, Ovid's **Metamorphoses**, and the philosophy of Boethius. She was quite taken up with Scholastic philosophy, mathematics, astronomy and especially music about which she seemed to exhibit technical knowledge. The subjects that interested her the most, however, were stories about Christ and legends of the saints. The passion with which she entered into these experiences is evidenced in her fervent and intense poetry.

Hroswitha's first writings were eight legends in verse. The first five were written with a preface dedicated to Gerberga which tells us much about the author. She tells her friend and mentor, "When you are weary, after your varied labors, deign to read these songs by way of play." She acknowledges that her work, "labored upon, with not little effort," be subjected to the criticism of "kindly and learned minds who take pleasure, not in exposing to ridicule a writer's faults but rather in correcting them." One wonders if she made a further comment with tongue in cheek. While admitting that some of the parts of her work were based on apocryphal or questionable materials, Hroswitha said she "declined to discard my subject matter, on the plea that what appears to be false may eventually be proved to be true." Right or wrong she was tenaciously loyal to her heroes and heroines! She may also be one of the first persons to recognize that basic truth can be found in the least likely sources.

Aware of how women were viewed in her day, outside the monastic milieu, Hroswitha wryly continues in the preface,

Even though the art of prosody may seem difficult and arduous for one of my feeble sex, nevertheless, relying in my own strength, I have attempted to sing the songs of this little collection...solicitous that the slight talent of ability given me by Heaven should not lie idle in the dark recesses of the mind and thus be destroyed by the rust of neglect... (all quotations taken from the translation of

**the preface found in Hroswitha of Gandersheim, edited
by Anne Lyon Haight, The Hroswitha Club, NY, 1965, pp.
13-15).**

The legends were dedicated to Gerberga II whom Hroswitha
addresses as the "illustrious offspring of a royal race." She praises
her for her character and learning and adds, "Fostering Mistress,
accept with kindliness these little verses..." (ibid., p. 15). The legends were written in poetic form and dealt with various subjects,
both overtly religious, such as those on the Virgin Mary and the
Ascension of the Lord, or more covertly religious, in those which
featured leaders, martyrs and fictional or mythological characters.

Hroswitha's most important original contributions to literature, however, are her dramas which have been produced on stage
from time to time in both European and American theaters. It is
not known if they were ever performed in her own day, but that
she intended them to be produced can be deduced from the stage
directions she attached to some of them. She followed the struc-
tural pattern of the plays of the pagan poet Terence but from an
entirely different point of view. The most obvious difference is
that she is a believer, but she was very much aware also of the
double standard existing for women in her day. Consequently,
unlike Terence, she made it a point to stress women's weaknesses
in such a clever way that, paradoxically, her readers' expectations
were foiled and the strength of women was emphasized instead.
Though she was in great admiration of Terence's style, her purpose for writing was to give Christian readers something good to
read as a substitution for the evil, though beautiful stylistic works
of the pagans. As she herself explains:

**I, the Strong Voice of Gandersheim, have not found it
objectionable to imitate him in composition, whom others study in reading, so that in that very form of composition through which the shameless acts of lascivious
women were depicted, the laudable chastity of sacred virgins may be praised within the limits of my little talent
(quoted in Medieval Women Writers, edited by Katharina**

M. Wilson, The University of Georgia Press, Athens, GA, 1984, p. 38).

The three subjects which preoccupied Hroswitha's thought and writings were her royal patrons (of Liudolf's dynasty), the Abbey of Gandersheim, and the Church, particularly in its ideal of chastity. In regard to the subject of chastity, one of her plays, **Dulcitius**, dramatizes her humor as well as demonstrating her ability in using Terence's style while accomplishing an entirely different aim. The story takes place during the persecutions of Diocletian and recounts the martyrdom of three virgin sisters. In it, Dulcitius, who appears as the devil, imprisons the girls in a room next to a pantry so that he can visit them at night. The fearful girls spend their time praying. When he comes in he is deluded into thinking the pots and pans in the kitchen are the sisters and so he embraces and kisses them instead. As a result, he comes out of the house smeared and blackened with soot, and the soldiers, who do not recognize him, chase him out of the palace. In this play, both virtue and comedy prevail!

The last of Hroswitha's works, still in existence, tells of the founding of her beloved monastery, Gandersheim. She relates that the site was chosen because of a mysterious apparition of lights in the depths of a forest. The swineherds in the field were the first to witness the wondrous sight, and then the owner of the homestead. Finally, Duke Liudolf heard about it:

> **And he himself, on holy Halloween,**
> **went with a crowd to keep vigil in that forest,**
> **keenly scanning to see if the apparition**
> **would again betoken something heavenly.**
> **At once, as thick night covered the land with mist,**
> **all around, circling the wooded valley**
> **where the surpassing noble temple was to be built,**
> **many lights were beheld, set in harmonious order:**
> **they cleft the tree-shadows, and the dark night too,**
> **with their radiantly penetrating gleam.**
> **All affirmed that this spot should be made holy,**

**in the service of him who had filled it with such light
(from Women Writers of the Middle Ages, edited by Peter
Dronke, Cambridge University Press, NY, 1984, p. 81).**

Just this small excerpt of her poem gives us a taste for the beauty
of Hroswitha's work!

HILDEGARD OF BINGEN

Earth Watcher

...then...that burning extends itself to a little clod of mud, which lies at the bottom of the atmosphere; this is to say that after the other creatures were created, the Word of God...considered the poor fragile matter from which the weak frailty of the human race, both bad and good, was to be produced, now lying in heavy unconsciousness and not yet roused by the breath of life; and warms it so that it is made flesh and blood—for earth is the fleshly material of humans—and nourished it with moisture, as a mother gives milk to her children; and blows upon it until it rises up a living human (Scivias, Vision I, #7).

Such is the earthy description of creation according to Hildegard of Bingen, mystic of the twelfth century. We could say she is one of the forerunners of contemporary creation theology as well as an advocate of the burning ecological issues of our day. Because of this, though not yet declared a "doctor of the Church" as was St. Catherine of Siena (fourteenth century) or St. Teresa of Avila (sixteenth century), this mystical writer is gaining increased attention in ecclesiastical circles today.

Hildegard was born in 1098 A.D. to Hildebert von Bermershein and Mechtilde near Alzey in Germany's beautiful Rhineland. Her parents, of upper nobility, tithed and consecrated her to God at

SCIVIAS

HILDEGARD of BINGEN

birth. When she was eight years old, they entrusted this tenth child to the hermitage of Jutta, daughter of the Count of Spanheim, whose family was closely connected with Hildegard's. This was not an unusual act as, at that time in Germany, Benedictine monasticism was an option for the elite. Under Jutta's tutelage she learned to read and write in Latin, to chant the monastic Office and to learn "women's domestic arts" such as spinning. She also studied the Rule of St. Benedict and the Fathers of the Church. One biographer said she learned from her mentor more by osmosis than in any systematic way. Later other young women joined the two and formed a community under Benedict's Rule. While still a teenager, Hildegard was clothed in the habit and made monastic profession. Little is known about her after that until 1136 when Jutta died and she succeeded her as abbess by unanimous vote.

Hildegard claimed to have had visions from her earliest age: "From my infancy until now, when I am seventy years of age, my soul has beheld this Light; and in it my soul soars to the summit of the firmament and into a different air..." This claim is found in a letter (Ep. 2) to Guibert of Gembloux, a Belgian monk, who was her secretary and friend for many years. Most of what we know of Hildegard's inner life comes from their correspondence compiled by two monks of Disibod and Echternach in a Vita. She described her visions as being reflections of the "living Light" and, in her letters to Guibert, she seems to have had a direct encounter with that Light. Elsewhere she described the concrete way she received these manifestations.

> **Truly I did not perceive these visions in dreams or sleeping, neither in a frenzy, nor with the bodily eyes or the outer ears, nor did I see them in remote places, but I received them waking and attentive with a clear mind, with my inner eyes and ears, in open places and according to the will of God (Scivias, opening declaration).**

The visions were accompanied by various illnesses that plagued her throughout life and she once told St. Bernard of Clairvaux they "burned" her soul. Current scholars have suggested her physical problems might have been caused by a form of migraine headache. Until modern times, the mystical leanings of visionaries were likely to be denigrated or scoffed at as the result of hysteria or neurosis. Despite her physical handicaps, Hildegard succeeded in living a very a very active life until her death September 17, 1179, still celebrated as her feast. The German people were so proud of their visionary they issued a postage stamp in 1979 commemorating the 800th anniversary of her death. Pope John Paul II has called her a prophetic sign, "an outstanding saint, a light to her time and [who] shines out more brightly today" ("Pope's Letter to Cardinal Volk, Bishop of Mainz," *L'Osservatore* Romano, Oct. 1, 1979, p. 10).

WORKS OF HILDEGARD

Hildegard was remarkable not only for her visions, but also for her extensive knowledge. A student of the usual subjects taught at the time, she was acquainted also with nature lore, describing in detail stones, trees, plants and especially the medicinal properties of herbs; she covered topics ranging all the way from nutrition to gynecology to emotional health. She wrote a scientific and medical encyclopedia titled **Nine Books on the Subtleties of Different Kinds of Creatures**, and a handbook of diseases, their symptoms and remedies, called **Book of Compound Medicine**. She was a politician, administrator, a preacher and was by some hailed as the "Sibyl of the Rhine" for her powers as a seeress and prophet. She wrote plays now performed by college drama departments, as well as liturgical songs (compiled under the title, **Symphony of the Harmony of Divine Revelations**) on the market today as recordings. She also wrote smaller works: a commentary on the Rule of Benedict, a biography of St. Disibod and one of St. Rupert, and homilies on the gospels of the liturgical year. Finally, more than three hundred letters attest to a wide range of correspondents from popes, emperors, abbesses and abbots, to clergy and laity.

However, it was shortly after she became abbess at Disbodenberg that Hildegard began a major trilogy, her visionary work, written under Divine command as she says in **Scivias** ("Know the Ways" of the Lord): "Write, therefore, the things you see and hear." **Scivias** was followed by **The Book of Life's Rewards** which, in allegorical style, deals with the virtues and vices. Completing the writings was the **Book of Divine Works** which deals with the relationship of the universe to humanity and a vision of future history. **Scivias** is the most famous. Divided into three parts, the first, with six visions, shows how the relationship of God, humanity and the world evolved; the second, with seven visions, centers on the stages of redemption; the third, with thirteen visions, presents an architectural image of salvation. The conclusion to **Scivias** depicts a revelation of the final days; thus, its entire scope ranges from creation to the apocalypse. She used striking, colorful imagery in her writings, so much so that she has been compared to Carl Jung for her ability to decipher the meaning behind symbols.

ACTIVITIES

About the same time she as writing **Scivias**, Hildegard became a public figure. She had a vision in which she was asked to found a monastery for her sisters at Rupertsberg near Bingen. Abbot Kuno and the monks of the Disibodenberg monastery were strongly against this idea. Immediately, Hildegard became seriously ill and remained so until the monks realized it was a sign from God that she was to build the new monastery. Rupertsberg flourished and Hildegard had the satisfaction of seeing it become independent from its founding house eventually. Before her death, however, she encountered a final sorrow when Rupertsberg was placed under interdict by the prelates of Mainz. This meant she and her sisters were denied the Eucharist, the sacraments and the Divine Office. Basically, there was a misunderstanding. She had allowed an excommunicated nobleman to be buried in the monastery cemetery. The prelates, acting in the absence of their archbishop, demanded that she exhume the body, which she refused to do. Eventually, Hildegard wrote to Archbishop

Christian in Rome explaining things, saying God in a vision had told her the young man had been properly reconciled to the Church. The archbishop, astute enough to know it was unwise to argue with someone as renowned as Hildegard, lifted the interdict.

This was not the only time Hildegard engaged in a spirited dialogue with authorities—this at a time preceding the outspoken St. Catherine of Siena by two centuries! As one scholar put it:

> **She castigated a pope for his timidity and an emperor for moral blindness. She taught scholars and preached to clergy and laity as no woman before her had ever done... It is difficult not to see in her visionary experience and activism, as well as her claim for the mission of woman in a male-dominated age, a gesture of protest, the reaction of an intelligent and energetic woman who chafed under the restraints imposed on women by the culture in which she lived (Bernard W. Scholz, "Hildegard von Bingen on the Nature of Woman," *The American Benedictine Review* December, 1980, p. 361).**

When Frederick (I) Barbarossa, formerly Hildegard's patron, participated in the appointment of Paschal III as anti-pope, she chided him in a letter which he did not answer. When Calixtus III was installed in 1168 as Paschal's successor she, undaunted, wrote again: "I through myself (God) destroy recalcitrance and crush the opposition of those who defy me. Woe, woe upon the evildoing of the unjust who scorn me! Hear this, king, if you would live— else my sword will pierce through you!" (quoted by Kent Kraft in Medieval Women Writers, ed. by Kathrine M. Wilson, University of Georgia Press, GA, 1984, p. 113). She was not at all sure Scivias would be accepted by Church officials. However, at the Synod of Trier in 1147, with Bernard of Clairvaux speaking on her behalf, Pope Eugenius III confirmed approval enthusiastically:

> **We are filled with admiration my daughter...for the new miracles that God has shown you in our time, filling you with his spirit so that you see, understand, and communicate many secret things. Reliable persons who have seen**

**and heard you, vouch to us for these facts. Guard and keep
this grace that is in you (quoted by Miriam Schmitt, O.S.B.
in 1986 Spring/Summer issue of *Benedictines*, p. 35).**

Bernard also expressed great respect for her in a letter: "We bless
the divine grace which resides in you... How can I aspire to
instruct and advise you, who have attained hidden knowledge
and in whom the influence of Christ's anointing still lives..."
(*ibid.*, pp. 35-36).

At age sixty she began a series of preaching tours. She traveled hundreds of miles to speak against the Cathari heresy and
for renewal among clergy and laity. Basically, however,
Hildegard was a contemplative, a woman of prayer. At the beginning of Scivias she said that in 1141, when she was

> **...forty-two and seven months old, heaven was opened
> and a fiery light of exceeding brilliance came and perme-
> ated my whole brain, and inflamed my whole heart and
> my whole breast, not like a burning but like a warming
> flame, as the sun warms anything its rays touch
> (Declaration before Vision I).**

Does Hildegard have any relevance for us today? As visionary,
feminist, healer, liturgist, ecumenist, cosmologist and ecologist
the answer can only be a resounding YES. Prayerfully in touch
with the living Light and maintaining a strong love for the
Church despite reprimands occasionally leveled at clerics, she
represents a positive voice for the issues which concern us. Some
quotations already cited above have indicated this, but a few
more will confirm her characteristic way of seeing things.

> **All nature is at the disposal of humankind.**
> **We are to work with it.**
> **Without it we cannot survive.**
>
> **The soul that is full of wisdom is saturated with the
> spray of a bubbling fountain—God himself.**

Like billowing clouds,
like the incessant gurgle of the brook,
the longing of the soul can never be stilled.

The human person is the form and the fullness of
creation.
In humankind, God brings to fullness all his creation.
God created humankind,
so that humankind might cultivate the earthly
and thereby create the heavenly.

BERNARD

The Last of the Fathers

Does St. Bernard of Clairvaux merit this title? Heaven forbid no other great writers and theologians deserve to be called a "Father of the Church" after this one. One only has to think, for example, of Meister Eckhart or John of the Cross, or perhaps Thomas Merton in our own day. No, it simply indicates the great respect writers and scholars have for this particular twelfth century monk who lived seven centuries after the period of the great ancient Fathers. To write about Bernard's life is to set oneself to the task of sorting out multitudinous events and of studying a complex personality. As Jean Leclercq, O.S.B., said, "We appreciate the fact that he is human, very human, but it is painful to find him so much a man at one time, while he appears so much a saint in other circumstances" (**Bernard of Clairvaux and the Cistercian Spirit**, Cistercian Publications, Kalamazoo, MI, 1976, p. 9).

Early biographical information is scarce. Bernard said nothing about his childhood and made only veiled references to temptations he experienced as an adolescent. The third of seven children, he was born in 1090 A.D. at Dijon, France and died on August 20, 1153 in his monastery of Clairvaux. His father, Tesceline, was a knight and his mother, Aleth, was from a noble family in Burgundy. That he had a good education under the Canons Regular is evident; his writings show he was a Latin classicist. Some have described him as a poet, artist and musician. Through his writings and comments made by historians we learn also that he had an aggressive personality while at the same time being pleasant enough to be able to draw others to himself. This ability is strongly demonstrated in the fact that he persuaded his uncle, all his brothers and a group of young noblemen to join his monastic way of life. He even convinced his only sister, Humbeline, to leave her husband and become a nun!

This leadership ability remained a constant throughout his life. In 1112 he entered Citeaux, a Cistercian monastery located only a few miles from where he was born, and three years later was sent to found a monastery at Clairvaux. Subsequently, he founded other monasteries, one after the other—sixty-eight of them in thirty-five years. By the time he died there were 350 houses belonging to the Cistercian Order, 164 more or less under his jurisdiction; they extended all over Europe reaching from Portugal to the south to Scandinavia in the north. Bernard's influence was not limited to monastic foundations however.

In 1127 or 1128 he was asked to write, "On the Conduct and Duties of Bishops," a sensitive assignment since abuses had crept in and his work would be read by his own archbishop. Nevertheless, he spoke with forthrightness and concern and his message was well received. Also, he was called upon to settle Church disputes. One of them led him to uphold the Knights Templar, a religious institute, whose duties, of protecting pilgrims to the Holy Land, sometimes involved fighting and killing others. His reasoning, based entirely on motivation, might cause us, sensitive about peace issues, to read his views with dismay. To his credit, he wrote a series of meditations for the Knights' use during their term of service near the Holy Places.

For eight years he was involved in working for Church unity when a schism was threatened by Anacletus II who tried to depose the legitimate pope, Innocent II. He traveled with the pope in France and Italy, attended the Council of Pisa in 1135 and, in 1137, the schism ended. All during this time he snatched moments to write on various topics. Because of his success in negotiating difficulties he increasingly became a public figure. In 1140 he was called upon to admonish a group of student clerics. Then he was urged by William of St. Thierry, a Cistercian at Clairvaux, to enter a controversy involving the teaching of Peter

Abelard, the famous teacher in the schools of Paris. This theological dispute became quite violent at times and finally was taken up in Rome. Looking from the vantage point of our hindsight, however, the writings of the two men actually clarified many issues for future theologians.

Though a real rivalry seems to have existed between Bernard and Peter Abelard, not so his relationship with Peter the Venerable, abbot of Cluny. Some scholars have tried to make a case that they were not true friends. However, twenty letters still in existence reveal a real friendship and affection between the two. Doubts about the genuineness of the relationship may stem from the difference in their personalities as well as the different approaches to monasticism taken by the Cluniac and Cistercian Orders. The friendship seems to have had a humanizing effect on Bernard and, in reverse, given Peter a more rigorous tendency as is evident in later Cluniac reforms. There is no question about his well-known friendship with William of St. Thierry and Aelred of Rievaulx.

In addition to being a healer of schism and entering into theological disputes, Bernard had one more disgression from his strictly monastic endeavors. Most school children have heard of the part he played in launching the second Crusade. He was requested to do so by King Louis VII of France and Eugene III, the first Cistercian pope, for the purpose of saving Christian holdings in the Holy Land from the infidels. A leader and ecumenist at heart, Bernard tried to unite the Christian rulers of east and west in his holy cause. Naive in the area of politics, his efforts did not stop the rivalries between sovereigns and knights and the enterprise fell apart. Unfortunately, Bernard was blamed for it entirely and this unpopularity affected his monasteries as well.

WRITINGS OF BERNARD

By far, Bernard's greatest influence centers around his writings. So copious and influential were they that he was named the "Doctor *Mellifluus*," that is, the one out of whom words flowed like honey. Like the early Church Fathers, he wrote treatises, sermons on the Song of Songs and on the liturgical year, saints' lives and so on. Unlike them, his works are more properly classified as "spiritual theology" rather than moral or dogmatic. Many historians consider him as a master of the spiritual life. A poet more than a teacher, he wrote imaginatively and symbolically and on every conceivable topic; consequently it is difficult to put his works in any kind of systematic order. Despite this difficulty we can find a single thread of unity in all his writings: he wrote from experience, from his interactions with the people and events of his time. His teachings, which reflect both his active and contemplative life, can best be found in his letters and his liturgical sermons. So can his concern for the welfare of his monasteries as, for example, in episcopal appointments, political conflicts and so on. It is said that he wrote over a thousand letters, more than five hundred of which are preserved.

Today scholars are still trying to interpret and unravel the richness of Bernard's thought which ranges anywhere from Plato's to Carl Jung's. His use of Scripture is not scientific. Simply stated, he sees the Bible as a love story between God and his people whether as Church or as individuals. His intention is to bring out the hidden rather than the literal meaning of the texts and so he uses highly symbolic images. Though specific quotations from the Fathers are rarely found in his writings, his dependence on their tradition flavors them.

One of his writings, **Five Books on Consideration**, deals with giving advice to Pope Eugene. A work of lesser importance, **Book on Precept and Dispensation**, concerned questions on monastic living raised by two Benedictine monks. His least known work, rarely translated, is the **Apologia**, a kind of digest of thought that resulted from the differences in Cluniac/Cistercian views on how to live the Rule of St. Benedict. Its importance lies in the fact that he wrote in frank terms to the monks of his own Order. Bernard's view is Christocentric; his rule of thumb: return to the early Fathers and see how they lived the life. The balance of his thought can be seen in this practical advice for the spiritual life: "There are people who go clad in tunics and have nothing to do with furs, who nevertheless are lacking in humility. Surely humility in furs is better than pride in tunics" (Basil Pennington, **The Last of the Fathers**, St. Bede's Publications, Still River, MA, 1983, p. 53).

Bernard's devotion to the Mother of God as expressed in his sermons, **In Praise of the Virgin Mary**, is famous. So popular was his mystical piety in her regard that it led to spectacular legends about him. One was that she had suckled him in infancy. Even Dante in his **Divine Comedy** required that Beatrice, his guide all through his journey, step aside for Bernard in order that he would be able to see the Blessed Virgin Mary standing before the face of God ("Il Paradiso," Canto XXXIII).

Most famous among his writings are **The Steps of Humility, On Loving God** and his sermons **On the Song of Songs**. In **The Steps of Humility** Bernard equates the steps with "steps of truth," inverting the twelve degrees of humility as found in the Rule of St. Benedict. Along with these steps, he shows their descending order and calls them "steps of pride." In his **On Loving God**, he is often remembered for his stating the idea that the measure of loving God is to love him without measure. Finally, the great regard Bernard had for Solomon's Canticle is revealed in his first sermon on that work which comprises five volumes. After commenting on the "shouts of joy and victory" and the "psalms and hymns and spiritual canticles" found in other parts of Scripture, he says:

But there is that other song which, by its unique dignity and sweetness, excels all those I have mentioned and any others there might be; hence, by every right do I acclaim it as the Song of Songs. It stands at a point where all the others culminate. Only the touch of the Spirit can inspire a song like this, and only personal experience can unfold its meaning. Let those who are versed in the mystery revel in it; let all others burn with desire rather to attain to this experience than merely to learn about it. For it is not a melody that resounds abroad but the very music of the heart, not a trilling on the lips but an inward pulsing

of delight, a harmony not of voices but of wills (On the Song of Songs, Book I, sermon 1).

ECOLOGIST FOR THE TWENTY-FIRST CENTURY

We turn up our noses at food that is unadulterated, as nature made it, and prefer to mix things together. We set aside their natural, God-given qualities so as to entice excess with hybrid delicacies. To take a single example: who could describe all the ways in which eggs are tampered with and tortured, or the care that goes into turning them one way and then turning them back? They might be cooked soft, hard, or scrambled. They might be fried or toasted, and occasionally they are stuffed. Sometimes they are served with other foods, and sometimes on their own. What reason can there be for all this variation except the gratification of a jaded appetite? A good deal of care is given to the appearance of a dish, so that the sense of sight is as much delighted by it as the palate. ...The eyes delight in colors, the palate in tastes, but the poor stomach can't see colors, and isn't tickled by tastes. It has to carry everything, and ends up being more oppressed than refreshed.

An Apologia to Abbot William

Jesus to me is honey in the mouth,
music in the ear,
a song in the heart.
Sermon 15, *On the Song of Songs*

MECHTILD

The Dancing Mystic

Of all the Mothers of the Faith, Mechtild of Magdeburg is perhaps the least traditional in the usual sense of the word. Born near Magdeburg in lower Saxony around 1207 A.D., she was blessed with many visions but, unlike other mystics of her day, over half her life was spent outside the sheltered environment of a family or a convent. Some say she was born of noble parentage; other authors express doubts about this. However, because of her references to courtly life and to the rich apparel of friends and relatives, most agree that she must have been wealthy and well-born. Her writings also give evidence to a cultured and refined background. Though very little is known of her family life, she claims, in her writings, that she was its "best loved" member. She may have had other siblings, but only one, Baldwin, is ever mentioned by name.

When she was twelve years of age, she had a "greeting" from the Holy Spirit which was repeated daily for thirty-one years. At age twenty-three she left her family and moved to the city of Magdeburg where she lived for forty years as a beguine. Though the group's origin is uncertain, the word "beguine" itself is derived from the name of Lamber le Begue, a priest of Liège, who counseled women to minister to the sick and the destitute. These women lived an austere and semi-religious community life, supporting themselves by begging, nursing, or the work of their hands. In the thirteenth century there were thousands of beguines in Germany and Belgium as well as some in other places on the continent. Not bound by vow, they could own property and were free to marry and to leave the community at any time. As a result, they attracted a wide variety of people—everyone from mystics to "loose women."

Obviously, in such an environment, Mechtild came into contact with many levels of society. The Dominican friars who came to Magdeburg in 1224 became her lifelong support. Her confessor, Henry of Halle, had been a student of Albert the Great. It was during this period of her life that Mechtild began the work which was to make her famous among the medieval writers—**The Flowing Light of the Godhead**. It is comprised of seven books, six of which were completed while she was with the beguines. The fourth book is semi-autobiographical and our main source of information on her life. The work is full of praise for the Dominicans. Some believed that she became a Dominican tertiary and that Baldwin was accepted into the Order because of the influence she exerted on his behalf. It is also quite possible that her Dominican confessor was instrumental in her eventual leaving of the beguines.

What is certain is that Henry of Halle can be credited for the writing of **The Flowing Light**, for in it she said, "he ordered a contemptible woman to write this book out of God's heart and mouth" (quoted from TFL, 4.2, in **Medieval Women Writers**, edited by Katharina M. Wilson, University of Georgia Press, 1984, p. 154). An account of her visions, it was written on loose sheets of paper which she then turned over to her confessor who compiled them into book form. Some of Mechtild's writings must have been circulated during her lifetime as, at one point, she was accused of heresy. Whether or not this is true is questionable, but it is easy to see why she roused the ire of some, especially the clergy. She denounced what she saw as abuses in the Church, using, with good reason, such terminology as "corrupt Christianity" or calling the Church a "maiden whose skin is filthy" (ibid., TFL, 5.34, p. 154). On an even more personal level she said that "God calls the cathedral clergy goats because their flesh stinks of impurity with regard to eternal truth..." (ibid., TFL, 6.3, p. 154).

Unfortunately, Mechtild, knowing the times in which she lived, felt it imperative to write in masculine terms so that any criticism directed at her writings would not be directed at her because she was a woman. When questioned by her compiler about the "masculine words" appearing in her book, she replied, "I wonder why that surprises you. But it grieves me more to the heart that I, a sinful woman, *must* so write" (ibid., TFL, 5.12, p. 155). It was a combination of such adverse circumstances that resulted in her leaving Magdeburg in 1270 for the monastery of Helfta near Eisleben in Saxony. The following passage gives us insight into the extent of Mechtild's lifelong suffering both mentally and physically:

> Not long after I came to the convent I became so painfully ill that my attendants had great pity for me. Then I spoke to our Lord: what do you want with this suffering? And our dear Lord said thus: all your paths are measured, all your footsteps counted, your life is blessed, your end will be happy, and my kingdom is very near you. —Lord, why is my life blessed, since I can do so little good? Then our Lord said: your life is sanctified because my rod has never left your back! (ibid., TFL, 7.4, p. 169).

Helfta was unique. In thirteenth century England all writings on mysticism were written by men, but on the continent they were written by nuns and it was this monastery which was the center of such writings. It is easy, therefore, to see why the abbess, Gertrude of Hackeborn, has been credited for heading one of the most productive and influential monasteries of the Middle Ages. She ruled from 1251-1291, and while she tried to maintain an environment conducive to contemplation, she insisted on rigorous study, especially of Scripture and of the arts—painting, music and writing. She collected books and had her nuns transcribe them. Her greatest fear was that if the pursuit of knowledge disappeared, Scripture would no longer be understood and this impoverishment would lead to an end of devotion as well.

The most famous people of Helfta in addition to the abbess, Gertrude of Hackeborn, were the sister of the abbess, Mechtild of Hackeborn; another Gertrude, later known as "the Great";

and, of course, Mechtild of Magdeburg. All these women were very gifted. The two bearing the name Mechtild were both writers and were contemporaneous with other writers of their time, including Dante. In fact, Mechtild of Hackeborn's description of heaven and Mechtild of Magdeburg's description of hell are very similar to those realities described in the **Divine Comedy**. In addition to her work on mysticism, Mechtild of Magdeburg made two unique contributions to the tradition of the Church. She was the first of the Christian mystics to write in her native tongue (German) rather than in the customary Latin. She was also the first to record a personal vision of the Sacred Heart, a cult which later became popularized with writings of Gertrude the Great.

We might think that Mechtild, a mystic, would be out of touch with practical living. Not so. Note how down to earth she is in this comment:

> **What hinders spiritual people most of all from complete perfection is that they pay so little attention to small sins. I tell you in truth: when I hold back a smile which would harm no one, or have a sourness in my heart which I tell to no one, or feel some impatience with my own pain, then my soul becomes so dark and my senses so dull and my heart so cold that I must weep greatly and lament pitiably and yearn greatly and humbly confess all my lack of virtue—for only then can I receive the blessing of being allowed to crawl back to the kitchen like a beaten dog (ibid., TFL, 5.33, p. 168).**

In another passage of her writings we find her admonishing the superiors:

> **You shall also go to the kitchen and see to it**
> **that the provisions for the sisters of the house are**
> **good enough**
> **that your thriftiness and the cook's laziness**
> **may not rob our Lord**
> **of sweet song in choir,**

for a hungry monk never sings well
and a hungry person cannot study deeply.
Thus might God often lose the best
because of the least
(quoted from TFL, 6.1, in The Women of Helfta by Mary
Jeremy Finnegan, O.P., The University of Georgia Press,
1991, pp. 19-20).

Or, even from the point of view of modern psychology, Mechtild
would be considered quite practical:

The fish in the water cannot drown,
The bird in the air cannot fall,
Gold is not destroyed by fire,
But there receives its shine and glow.
God has given to all creatures
The way to follow their own nature.
How then could I resist my nature?
(quoted in Women Mystics in Medieval Europe by Emilie
Zum Brunn and Georgette Epiney-Burgard, Paragon House,
NY, 1989, p. 59).

Her "nature," of course, was to leave all things to follow God.

Mechtild, though she spent only twelve years in Helfta, made a
great contribution to the monastery. She herself, however, felt
she was useless to the community. After suffering illnesses
throughout her life and enduring years of austerities and mental
suffering as a beguine, she underwent another serious illness
shortly after arriving which left her blind. The nuns, however,
received her joyfully and often went to her for advice. Mechtild
was surprised at this and one time expressed her great gratitude
to them:

...Lord, I thank you that since in your love you have taken
from me all earthly riches, you now clothe and feed me
through the goodness of others.... Lord, I thank you that
since you have taken from me the sight of my eyes, you

**serve me through the eyes of others. Lord, I thank you
that since you have taken from me the strength of my
hands...and the strength of my heart, you now serve me
with the hands and hearts of others. Lord, I pray you for
them (quoted from TFL, 7.64 in Finnegan, op. cit., p. 16)**

As for her work, **The Flowing Light of the Godhead** included
many forms of writing: lyric, dialogue, prose narrative. These
forms were used to write prayers, meditations, reflections on the
times and short accounts of spiritual visions. Though Mechtild's
writings incurred the wrath of the clergy, they endeared her to
the nuns. It is easy to understand why. They portray a woman
deeply in love with God and with whom she enjoyed an intimate
relationship. Notice this for example:

**I cannot dance, O Lord, unless you lead me.
If I leap high joyfully, you yourself must first leap
and sing—
Then I too shall leap with love,
From love to knowledge,
From knowledge to fulfillment,
From fulfillment to beyond all human senses
(ibid., TFL, 1.44, p. 18).**

The dance, as an image, originated from a period after the
philosopher Plato which was later adopted by Catholic mysticism. Mechtild unites the image with the contemporary courtly
custom of the spring dance. In book 1.44, Christ appears to her
in the form of a noble youth. He and the virtues take part in a
blessed dance and ask Mechtild to join them. Jesus answers the
quotation cited above by saying, "Madam, in this dance of praise,
you have done well" (quoted in Finnegan, op. cit., p. 18).

It may be a consolation for many of us to know that Mechtild,
despite her intimacy with God, had to struggle with pain and was
apprehensive all her life about the kind of death she would have.
In one of her visions God told her: "When that happens, I will
draw my breath and you will come to me as to a magnet" (quoted

from TFL, 5.32, in Wilson, op. cit., p. 156). Abbess Gertrude who was present at her death confirmed that it was, indeed, both dignified and serene. Afterward the abbess prayed for a sign to occur so as to silence Mechtild's critics, but God let her know that miracles were not necessary to demonstrate Christ's victories.

Mechtild herself must have had confidence that her writings would live on after her death as she wrote: "Any honest woman or good man who would have liked to speak with me and after my death cannot do so, should read this little book" (quoted from TFL, 6.1, in Finnegan, op. cit., p. 22). One of her visions seemed to have brought her this assurance from a source greater than herself. When saddened by the prediction that her writings would one day be burned by her critics, she complained she had been misled by God who had told her to write them. She adds,

Then God revealed Himself at once
to my sad soul and held this book in His extended hand
and said: My dear, do not be too sad:
no one may burn the truth.
The one who would take it from My hand
must be stronger than I!
(quoted from TFL, 2.26, in Wilson, op. cit., p. 164).

Finally, in closing this account of the life of Mechtild of Magdeburg, we might like to consider using one little phrase from **The Flowing Light** as our own daily mantra or prayer. In its brevity and lilt does it not seem to have a slightly Irish ring to it?

His eyes in my eyes
His heart in my heart
His soul in my soul
Enclosed and at peace
(quoted from TFL, 2.4, in Finnegan, op. cit., p. 18).

GERTRUDE
THE GREAT

Heart to Heart

A saint particularly dear to the heart of Benedictines and the first female saint honored with the title, "Great," is St. Gertrude of Helfta, Germany. For the most part, authors agree she was born January 5, 1256, but they differ on the date of her death, placed between 1301-1303. Despite this rather exact information, writers say almost nothing regarding her family or place of birth, though one claims she belonged to a noble house of the Counts of Lachenborn in Saxony. She may have been orphaned, but the first durable historical fact we have about her is that she was confided to the nuns at the Helfta monastery when she was five years of age and there she was raised and educated. Some say she had determined to consecrate herself to Christ as his bride at this young age.

It is not certain if the monastery was Benedictine or Cistercian. Gertrude of Hackeborn was abbess at Helfta at the time. The similarity of their names led to the erroneous belief that St. Gertrude had been the abbess at one time. The young girl was entrusted to the care of the abbess' sister, St. Mechtild, fifteen to twenty years her senior. To situate St. Gertrude historically, she lived at the time when the Dominicans, Franciscans and Carmelites came into being. The thirteenth century was also the period of Albert the Great and King St. Louis.

In school the children loved her for her gentle, kind ways. Though described as "lovable, clever and talkative," she loved

211

silence and solitude. Gertrude studied Latin, philosophy and theology. In fact she became so engrossed in these studies that she was hindered in prayer. We are told Jesus himself pointed out this fault to her. Later, in her first visionary experience at age twenty-five or six, he showed himself to her as a young boy of about sixteen. He let her know he had forgiven her this fault and from then on she practiced continual remembrance of the presence of God. She never lost a sense of this presence.

The friendship which developed between her mentor, St. Mechtild, and herself proved a great boon for St. Gertrude. They became soul friends who confided in each other and helped each other in moments of trial. Because of her holiness and her discernment of spirits, the abbess encouraged the nuns to seek Gertrude's advice. She was reluctant to speak of the favors she received from the Lord. Nevertheless, they were revealed to St. Mechtild by Jesus. He let her know of Gertrude's state of perfection and of her constant attentiveness to the presence of God. He told her that there was no dwelling place so pleasing to him as the heart of Gertrude. It is possible that this was the reason the title "Great" was given to her. Once she did admit receiving a special grace given on one of the Sundays after Pentecost:

You invited me to such a union with yourself that I marveled, more than at a miracle...the fact that I was able once more to live as a human among humans (Revelations 2, 23).

The Office of Gertrude's feast (November 16) tells us that Christ was in the habit of speaking to his beloved Gertrude "face to face as one is accustomed to speak to a friend." The words, of course, are lifted from the words of Sacred Scripture which describe the familiar relationship Moses enjoyed with God; however, they are most applicable to her. Most of the visions this great contemplative enjoyed were in some way connected to the liturgical feasts, particularly the feast of Christmas. She was born on the feast of the Epiphany which is within the Christmas cycle and her first vision took place in Advent when Jesus came to her, as she expressed it, as the "Dayspring from on high."

GERTRUDE
THE
GREAT

During another Christmas vision she experienced the Blessed Mother placing the Infant Jesus in her arms:

...your spotless mother proffered me, with her spotless hand, you the child of her virginity, a lovely little baby struggling with all his might to be embraced by me...you clung to me with your little arms (Revelations 2, 158).

A contemporary writer, Sister Lillian Thomas Shank, O.C.S.O., says that Christmas was a powerful incentive in Gertrude's spirituality and that she implied in various ways through visions that every day is Christmas for the person who is seriously seeking God.

The liturgy formed her spirituality and from it she drew the major emphases of her spiritual teachings and doctrine. She together with Mechtild (sometimes called "of Hackeborn" to distinguish her from the famous Mechtild of Magdeburg), were most influential in directing the contemplation of the nuns. Forbidden by the age in which she lived to give sermons or write commentaries on disputed theological questions, Gertrude, like Julian of Norwich in the next century, hid her teachings in letters, prayers or writings in the form of visions, that is, personal formulations of devotion which, in turn, gave theological direction to the prayers of her readers. Despite the fact that most of Gertrude's spirituality is within the context of liturgy, she was not entirely unacquainted with matters of social consciousness. The miracles attributed to her were the result of her compassion for the poor and suffering: rain when it was needed for the farmers and the ceasing of rain when it threatened their harvest and so on.

Her writings are very few. Of the five books in **The Herald of Divine Love** (more commonly known as the **Revelations**), it is certain that only Book II was written by Gertrude. The others seem to have been written by someone in whom she confided. There is even more uncertainty regarding the **Prayers of St. Gertrude**. A small **Book of Special Grace** on the graces received by St. Mechtild also has been attributed to her. It is likely she did this jointly with someone else. **The Spiritual Exercises** bears the most solid attribution of authorship and is the book most widely read. These **Exercises** were used by some Benedictine Sisters in the United States as their Divine Office until replaced by the Office of the Blessed Virgin Mary and, finally, the monastic Liturgy of the Hours used today. Lost completely are her writings and commentaries on Scripture and the sermons of the Fathers.

Gertrude's effusive language is foreign to our way of speaking. However, if we consider that prior to age thirty-four she did not remember ever having seen a mother caressing her child, her vocabulary seems remarkably rich. Note, for example, the titles she gives Jesus: "...O serenest light, utmost bright morning...O my most dulcet morning...flowering spring day filled with life...oak of hope" and so on. Or one of her prayers in honor of the wounds of Christ:

Glory be to you, most sweet, most gentle, resplendent and ever placid, most mirthful and most glorious Trinity, for the rosy wounds of my only Beloved (Revelations 4, 35).

We can say that the beginnings of the Sacred Heart devotion, later promulgated officially with St. Margaret Mary Alacoque, originated with St. Gertrude. This was the sign of the intimate union Jesus chose to maintain with her: "I give you my Heart...that it may supply all your incapacities... Make use of it and your works will charm the eye and the ear of the Divinity." In her **Exercises** a mutual exchange takes place as she says: "O let there be opened to me the saving entry into your most dear Heart. See my heart; I want to possess it no longer, but you take it, my dearest treasure and keep it with you in your safe place."

May St. Gertrude's wish be fulfilled in all of us:

I long to praise you so that some people who read this account may take delight in the sweetness of your intimacy, and under this inducement may achieve personal experience in their inmost being of ampler graces...may they be led by these pictures I have painted...to taste within themselves that hidden manna (Revelations 2, 198).

JULIAN OF NORWICH

God as Mother

Julian of Norwich, who lived in fourteenth century England, was quite taken up with the image of God as Mother. This can shock anyone not familiar with passages from the Old Testament which depict God in this way as, for example, in Isaiah:

> Can a mother forget her infant,
>   be without tenderness for the child of her womb?
> Even should she forget,
>   I will never forget you (49:15).

Or Hosea: "I drew them with human cords; I fostered them like one who raises an infant to the cheek" (11:4). Julian, unlike her contemporary, St. Catherine of Siena, who was greatly involved in the political life of her Church and country, was a recluse so hidden from human sight as to have her historical identity all but lost. Margery Kempe, a lay woman, tells in her **Book** that she had visited Julian in her cell as to an expert in spiritual matters. However, it is evident in Kempe's writings that Julian never told her about her visions or that she had written about them.

This visionary lived the solitary and enclosed life of an anchoress (with a maid servant as was the custom) in a cell adjoining the parish church of St. Julian in Conisford at Norwich. The church still stands though the cell, destroyed in

World War II, is a reconstruction. We know nothing about her life except what she tells in her **Revelations** or **Showings of the Love of God** as it is sometimes called. We are not even certain "Julian" was her given name as it was customary for an anchoress to adopt the name of the church to which she was attached. She speaks of being thirty and a half years old on May 8, 1373, which would make her birthdate sometime in December, 1342. Her date of death is uncertain, though from references of people who visited her cell at various times we find she lived until she was about eighty.

Despite the lack of biographical information, we know she lived at a time of great hostilities between France and Scotland as well as the time of the Avignon Papacy, the Black Death and the beginning of the Hundred Years' War. Her parentage is unknown though she does speak of her mother being at her bedside when it was thought she was dying. One writer suggests that her natural and spontaneous delight in God indicates she had a happy childhood. Others are led to believe her familiarity with colors and textures of cloth indicates her family dealt in the wool or cloth trade of the day.

The suppositions we have regarding her education are partly gleaned from the content and style of her writing and her association with the educated Benedictine women at nearby Carrow. From this association some writers further conclude she was drawn to contemplative life and entered a religious order at a young age. If so, it would give additional credence to the academic training. About her contemplative bent, some suggest that Julian's words, "This book is begun by God's gift and his grace but it is not yet performed" (**Showings**, Ch. 86), show that she intended, after its completion, to devote herself to a more contemplative form of living. The fact that she began the more severe life of a solitary a year after she finished her work supports this belief.

In her writings she claims she is an ignorant person lacking writing skills, but it is clear she is using a common rhetorical device. Though she did lack literary skills when she first received her revelations she soon became proficient in them. Some

authors have compared her to Geoffrey Chaucer, whose translation of Boethius' **Consolation of Philosophy** was written about
the same time. A more modern writer, Evelyn Underhill, was
bold enough to call her "the first English woman of letters."
Julian's style points to a familiarity with classical spiritual writings of the contemplative monastic tradition, especially those of
William of St. Thierry.

Her works, though showing a likeness in doctrine with William
of St. Thierry's, received much more adverse criticism and fewer
of her works have been preserved for us than his or Walter
Hilton's, another contemporary. We could conjecture that this
was due to sexism, more effectively exposed today. Consequently,
Julian's work received only limited circulation for three centuries.
The text was not written in a popularized style nor did it flow
smoothly as some mediaeval writings; further, few editors in her
time were willing to work with it. Unique to her writings was the
description of a near death experience and, though she told her
visions with utter simplicity, they contained several levels of
meaning which puzzle scholars even today. Those who make a
study of Julian's writings have two texts to work from—her first
draft the **Short Text**, and a final one, the **Long Text**.

It was not until 1388 A.D. or later that Julian understood totally the revelations she received; hence, the **Long Text** written
twenty years later. Psychologically, we can see a change in attitude when comparing the two texts: from a more individualized
approach to a more universal one; toward a more compassionate
understanding of the failures of human beings; toward a branch-
ing out to wider theological interests. As far as the content goes,
Julian's first revelation tells us that, at the age of fifteen she
asked for the grace to contract a sickness which might appear to
be fatal to herself and to all others, and for the gift of three
"wounds"—true contrition, loving compassion and a longing will
for God. She was granted the sickness at the time requested (her
thirtieth year) and it was followed by a miraculous cure. Both
were preparations for the revelations to follow. She also received
three graces: the cure, an impulse to pray once again for the second wound, and a glimpse of Christ's head bleeding under the

crown of thorns. This sight, instead of filling her with sadness, brought on a sudden delight: "...the Trinity filled my heart with the greatest joy..." (Ch. 4), for by it, Christ made her understand that the Trinity is our protector, lover, our joy and bliss. Later when she realized what Christ's Passion accomplished for us, she says,

> ...I laughed greatly, and that made those around me to laugh as well; and their laughter was pleasing to me. ...I wished that all my fellow Christians had seen what I saw. Then they would all have laughed with me. But I did not see Christ laugh; nevertheless, it is pleasing to him that we laugh to comfort ourselves, and that we rejoice in God because the devil is overcome (Ch. 8).

Unlike earlier writers and, indeed, her contemporaries, with the single exception of Meister Eckhart, she did not see the spiritual life as a hard and rugged way of climbing some "ladder of perfection," or the difficult practicing of virtues. Rather, her stress, more feminine, is the non-competitive, non-compulsive way of basking in God's goodness and having compassion for all his creation.

> I understood that the Lord looks on his servants with pity and not with blame...In God's sight we do not fall; in our sight we do not stand. As I see it both of these are true. But the deeper insight belongs to God (Chs. 80 and 82).

Neither did she emphasize the separation of body and soul as so many spiritual writers do. Instead, she speaks of wholeness and unity—integration—calling God the "still point at the center" (Ch. 11). For Julian, Christ does not come to "take away sin"; his work is a bringing together, a "one-ing" of himself with us to heal us.

> All the gifts which God can give to the creature he has given to his son Jesus for us, which gifts he, dwelling in us, has enclosed in him until the time that we are fully

grown, our soul together with our body and our body together with our soul (Ch. 55).

In the **Long Text** Julian's allegory of the lord and servant shows her obsession with the problem of God's relationship with us: how can sin, damnation and the anger of God be reconciled with his mercy and grace? It is resolved in the chapters in which she describes her trust in God through the image of a child's relationship to its parents, especially to its mother:

> As truly as God is our father, so just as truly is he our mother...In our Father, God Almighty, we have our being; in our merciful mother we are remade and restored. Our fragmented lives are knit together and made perfect...and by giving and yielding ourselves, through grace, to the Holy Spirit we are made whole (Chs. 58 and 59). Because of our good Lord's tender love to all those who shall be saved, he quickly comforts them, saying, 'The cause of all this pain is sin. But all shall be well, and all shall be well, and all manner of thing shall be well.' (Ch. 27).

Jesus, too, is described by Julian as mother:

> As we know, our own mother bore us only into pain and dying. But our true mother Jesus, who is all love, bears us into joy and endless living. Blessed may he be! ...A mother feeds her child with her milk, but our beloved mother Jesus feeds us with himself...the most treasured food of life (Ch. 60).

Finally, we can say that she is unique in her expression of a cosmic, creation-centered spirituality.

> He showed me a little thing, the size of a hazelnut, in the palm of my hand, and it was round as a ball. I looked at it with my mind's eye and thought, 'What can this be?'

And answer came, 'It is all that is made.' I marveled that it could last, for I thought it might have crumbled to nothing, it was so small. And the answer came into my mind, 'It lasts and ever shall because God loves it.' And all things have being through the love of God (Ch. 5).

To use a pun, Julian "wraps up her teaching in a nutshell!" On May 8, 1980, the Church of England first celebrated Julian as a saint.

CATHERINE
OF SIENA

A Liberated Woman

The story of St. Catherine of Siena is one of a liberated woman. It provides a taste of the women's movement long before the urgency that movement has assumed today. It is also a story which can give us hope in our constant struggle to balance a life of prayer with activity. A biography, written by her confessor Raymond of Capua, claims "...there is in my narrative neither fiction nor falsehood, and the facts are as faithfully reported as my weakness would allow" (**Life of Saint Catherine of Siena**, P.J. Kenedy & Sons, NY, 1853, p. 20). This is perhaps true. What is also clear is that one of his weaknesses, an exaggerated admiration of Catherine, resulted in some embellishment of his stylistic account. However, Raymond does give some interesting details often lost to us in the lives of most saints.

Catherine was born in Siena in 1347, the twenty-fourth child of twenty-five, to her father Jacoma Benincasa, a wool dyer of comfortable means, and her mother Lapa (meaning, "the fruitful bee"). A twin sister died in infancy. One of the stories told by Raymond, though considered pious legend by some historians, was that at the age of six, while going on an errand with her brother, she had a vision of Jesus, in bishop's robes, accompanied by Sts. Peter, Paul and John the Evangelist. However true the story, we know she vowed her virginity to God at age seven. At fifteen, considered marriageable age, she cut off her hair in

CATHERINE OF SIENA

defiance of the attempts of relatives to increase her attractiveness. She did not do this, however, without emotional struggle. She loved to hear about the Fathers of the Church and, in imitation of the early desert Fathers, attempted to withdraw to a hermitage and live a life of solitude. God made it known this was not to be her life-style. Her family lived near the church and cloister of a Dominican center of learning and eventually Catherine, at eighteen, joined the "mantellate," affiliated with this group.

From this time on she began to live a life of solitude combined with serving the destitute and sick of Siena. People from all walks of life and religious persuasions sought her out at home. This resulted in her engaging in theological argumentation and biblical interpretation and sharing the teaching she derived from her experiential encounters with God. These gatherings were not unlike our modern discussion groups. A pleasant, outgoing and idealistic person, Catherine was independent and had a passion for truth which later came out strongly in her writings. God, for her, was "the gentle first Truth." The year 1370 marks the climax of her mystical experiences. Described as the "mystical death," for four hours she experienced union with God in such a way that to outsiders she appeared dead. After that her austerity led her to practice almost total abstinence from food and sleep.

Catherine lived in an age when society in general was in chaos; the Church and the Dominicans did not remain untouched. In Siena she felt called to counsel others in addition to praying for them. Her efforts to offset some of the tensions between the city-states and the papacy led to several trips away from home. A journey to Florence occasioned her first meeting with Raymond of Capua who became a lifelong friend. As Catherine described the relationship, he was "the father and son given to me by that gentle Mother Mary." Truth to tell, she advised him as much as he advised her. In the same year (1374) there was a second outbreak of the bubonic plague known as the "Black Death." Before it ended the Benincasa family itself lost eight members. In Pisa Catherine used her influence to divert the people from making an alliance with an anti-papal league. It was here, too, that she received the stigmata, visible only to herself at her own request.

The time in which Catherine lived is a study in contrasts. A century of the great mystics—Meister Eckhart, John Tauler, Blessed Suso, Julian of Norwich—it was also the dark age of the Church known as the "Avignon Papacy" (also called the "Babylonian Captivity") when the pope lived luxuriously in Avignon, France, rather than in Rome. He, a Frenchman, also lived at the mercy of the French dynasty. During this time Catherine attempted, at the pope's request, to bring about a reconciliation between the papacy and the Florentines, but they wanted peace on their own terms. The second time he sent her to them she was almost assassinated; when martyrdom escaped her she cried. After that she gave her attention to her three great concerns: the reformation of the clergy, the Crusade and the return of the papacy to Rome. In regard to the first, Catherine admonished Pope Gregory XI, "...you must pluck out of the garden of Holy Church those flowers that spread the infection of impurity, avarice and pride: that is to say, the bad pastors and superiors who poison and corrupt this garden" (Letter 206). About the second concern, she did not think it bold to write to Charles V, King of France, "Do God's will and mine" asking him to take part in the Crusade. To solve the final issue Catherine addressed Gregory XI as "sweetest Babbo ('Daddy') mine" and wrote:

> **Come and do not resist any longer the will of God who calls you. Your hungry sheep wait for you to come to take and keep the place of your predecessor and leader, the apostle St. Peter. Your office as Vicar of Christ obliges you to live in your proper place. Come, then, come! Do not delay any longer! Take courage and do not fear what may befall you, because God will be with you! (Letter 197).**

This fourteenth century woman was no shrinking violet before her male counterparts!

After the pope's return to Rome she founded a women's monastery of strict observance outside Siena in 1377. Raymond of Capua was assigned to Rome at this time, but to make up for this loss, she was blessed by God with a spiritual encounter which led her to write her most famous work, **The Dialogue**. She did not limit her speaking and writing to clergy and kings. She also influenced abbots, laity, mercenaries, prostitutes and prisoners. A most touching incident in her life concerns a Perugian nobleman, Nicolo Toldo, who was condemned to death for speaking against the Republic. When a priest came to comfort him, the young man, infuriated, blasphemed God for allowing him to die unjustly. After a visit from Catherine, however, he became so resigned that he asked her to be present at his execution. When the time came, she bared his neck for the executioner's blow and Nicolo smiled, asking her to make the sign of the cross over him. He died with both the name of Jesus and Catherine on his lips.

When Gregory XI died, Urban VI was elected pope. He was so opposed by some groups that schism was threatened. He sent for Catherine but, it turned out, her efforts were to no avail and the "Great Schism" of the Church, when a second pope was elected to oppose the true pope, Urban VI, occurred. While in Rome, Catherine set up a small household of women and men who lived on alms. From 1380 on she could not eat or even swallow water. Her activity, after that, was centered entirely on prayer. She died on Ascension Thursday, April 29 that year, a date still celebrated as her feast in the Church. On October 4, 1970, Pope Paul VI declared her a Doctor of the Church, an honor shared with only one other woman, Teresa of Avila.

MYSTICISM AND WORKS OF CATHERINE

The account of her **Life** tells us that 1368 marked the year of Catherine's mystical marriage to Jesus. Raymond says the Mother of God presented her to her Son, who offered her a golden ring containing four precious stones with a diamond in the center saying:

I your Creator and Redeemer espouse you in faith and you shall preserve it (i.e. this espousal represented by the ring) pure until we celebrate together in heaven the

eternal nuptials of the Lamb. Daughter, act courageously; accomplish without fear the work that my Providence will confide to you; you are armed with faith, you shall triumph over all your enemies (p. 76).

One day in 1370 when she was petitioning God to give her the spirit of a new heart, she seemed to experience Jesus opening her left side, removing her heart and taking it with him. A few days later she was enveloped in light and saw Jesus opening her side again, this time to insert his own heart which he told her would serve her from then on.

To those of us who live in a technocratic society, the extraordinary favors—raptures, ecstasies, conversations and so on—given to Catherine in prayer may sound unreal or extreme. However, the last twelve years of her life reveal that she did not find any difficulty maintaining the balance between contemplation/ action that we do. She did not pray to get strength for action; her prayer moved her to act. Her **Life** tells us Jesus once said, "Daughter, think of me and I will think continually of you" (p. 63). This she did no matter how involved she was with activities. She counseled Raymond in a similar vein to do the same: "You will rarely have the joy of being in your monastic cell, but I wish you always to carry around with you the cell of your heart..." (Letter 373).

Up to the time she wrote **The Dialogue** she had always written by way of dictation. Miraculously, at age thirty, she learned to write. In addition to this work, she wrote about four hundred letters and a dozen prayers. We find in her writings the influence of the Fathers of the Church—among them Augustine, Cassian, Gregory the Great and Bernard. **The Dialogue** shows us that she was very orthodox in teaching while displaying a certain originality in the way she expressed herself. A familiarity with the Bible is indicated in the way her own thoughts were intertwined with Sacred Scripture—so closely in fact that her sentences are hard to punctuate. Scholars have had a difficult time translating **The Dialogue** because she spoke just as the words came to her in ecstasy. Though some of it was dictated while in ecstasy,

Catherine did write and edit some of the work herself. Trying to explain herself in parentheses along the way both helped and confused later editors. Writers have tried, with little success, to re-organize and outline the work to make it more understandable. These writers say her work is basically comprised of the following pattern: four petitions to God (for herself, for the reform of the Church, for the whole world and for a certain unnamed sinner), each followed by God's response to her.

Catherine's letters give us more insight into her colorful personality as well as her own growth. They also seem more practical to us moderns and remind us that she was not just caught up in lofty matter of state or in raptures and ecstasies. Even in **The Dialogue** we sometimes see how firmly she had her feet on the ground when it came to human relations. The following passage, often quoted as a general favorite by writers of spirituality, can help us in our own struggling efforts in this area. It also gives us a sample of Catherine's own peculiar "logic." Jesus is speaking to her:

> I require that you should love me with the same love with which I love you. This indeed you cannot do, because I loved you without being loved. All the love which you have for me you owe to me, so that it is not of grace that you love me but because you ought to do so. On the other hand, I love you of grace and not because I owe you my love.
>
> Therefore to me in person you cannot repay the love which I require of you. I have, then, placed you in the midst of other human beings that you may do to them that which you cannot do to me, that is to say, that you may love your neighbor of free grace without expecting any return from them, and what you do to them I count as done to me (The Dialogue, chapter 89).

TERESA
OF AVILA

Daughter of the Church

Teresa of Avila, sometimes called the "big" Teresa to distinguish her from the "Little Flower," was born on March 28, 1515 in Avila, which is located in the Castilian region of Spain. After the death of his first wife, her father, Don Alonso Sanches de Cedpeda, married Doña Beatriz de Ahumada. Teresa was one of ten children from this second marriage. Her parents, pious and good, taught their children to pray and to be charitable to the poor. Family recitation of the rosary after supper every evening acquainted Teresa with the life of Christ. In early childhood she was filled with a desire to bring all people to God through imitating the saints by suffering with Christ. So strong was this desire that, at seven, she convinced her favorite brother, Rodrigo, eleven, they should die as martyrs so they could enter heaven immediately. Deciding to go to Africa, they anticipated martyrdom at the hands of the Moors. Fortunately, by chance, their uncle, on horseback, met them on the way and intercepted these plans.

Teresa's family, on both sides, boasted their blood was untainted by any Moorish or Jewish blood. Later, Teresa countered this obvious prejudice of her day by saying, "It is enough for me to be a daughter of the Church; it would trouble me more to have committed a venial sin than to be descended from the lowest and vilest people in the world" (**St. Teresa of Avila** by William T. Walsh, Bruce Publishing Co., Milwaukee, WI, 1943, p. 5). Her

Teresa
of
Avila

mother died when she was twelve and two years later her father sent her to a school run by Augustinian nuns. Though deeply religious, he was dismayed when his favorite daughter expressed, as a result of this association, an attraction to religious life. Nevertheless, Teresa, after reading the **Letters** of St. Jerome, decided to leave home and, on November 2, 1535, she entered the Carmelite monastery in Avila. She felt the separation from her father keenly, but was ecstatic when he, realizing how determined she was in her resolve, finally acquiesced to her wishes. In 1538 she made her profession of vows, shortly after which she became so seriously ill that a female healer was called in. Her treatment almost resulted in Teresa's death. After a three-day coma she revived but was left paralyzed and unable to walk for three years. Attributing her cure to St. Joseph, she experienced the effects of this illness for the rest of her life.

As a child, Teresa loved to dress up and wear makeup and some of this "frivolity" remained with her when she entered the monastery. However, she soon questioned the comfortable lifestyle of her convent and one of her visions—of hell—gave her a determination to live out the Carmelite tradition more perfectly. To accomplish this task, she started a new foundation in 1562, the monastery of St. Joseph, in Avila. To help her nuns, she began to write doctrinal and practical instructions on the life of prayer. This compilation was eventually titled the **Way of Perfection**, considered a spiritual classic today. The foundation and her book, however, were only a beginning. When Father Rubo, the superior general of the Carmelite Order, visited her monastery in 1567, he was so pleased by it that he asked her to found as many of these monasteries as she could. She soon enlisted St. John of the Cross to found similar monasteries for the Carmelite friars. Before she died she had fourteen monasteries to her credit, all described in her work, the **Book of Foundations**.

The phenomenal success of Teresa's work should not give the impression her life was easy. She had many struggles both within herself and on the outside from others. Some people misunderstood her and some, not wanting to be reformed, gave endless opposition to her monasteries. Trials, however, brought out the best in this very independent, intelligent and enterprising woman. Traveling to found monasteries brought her into contact with a broad range of society—from the poor to the nobility. Like Catherine of Siena, she was involved with rulers (King Philip II and the Duke of Alba particularly), threats of war between nations (Spain and Portugal), legal disputes within her own family and with quarrels between the Spanish government and Rome. She educated herself through continuous reading and talking to learned people. Not accepting the prevailing view that only men were capable of serious thought, she entered into discussion with them. Complaining to the Lord once she said she felt it unfair that "strong, serene, confident hearts" should be despised only because they belonged to women. Despite all her activity, she was able to carry on a vast correspondence not only with the parties involved in the problems above, but also to those seeking her advice on a wide range of issues, particularly in regard to her monastic foundations. Her warmth and charm won many to her cause. The strain of terrible traveling conditions and frequent illnesses literally fatigued her to death. She died on October 4, 1582 as she was reciting verses from the **Song of Songs**. On September 27, 1970, Pope Paul VI proclaimed her a Doctor of the Church.

An account of Teresa's external life is to tell only half the story; indeed, the least important half. The journeys she took to found her Carmels were nothing compared to her journeys in the spirit. Her title "Doctor" was earned by her descriptions of her mystical experiences which, even today, are considered masterpieces. All of her writings originated from obedience to her confessors or prelates who asked her to record her experiences. Despite the exalted character of her prayer life, Teresa was very practical and down to earth especially in her descriptions of community life. To those who regarded the life of perfection as being one of conformity to rules, she said such conformity

...will not bring many souls to God because they will see so much repression and tenseness. Our nature is such that this constraint is frightening and oppressive to oth-

ers, and they flee from following the road you are taking, even though they know clearly that it is the more virtuous path (Way of Perfection, Ch. 41).

St. Gregory the Great's **Morals** and the **Third Spiritual Alphabet** by a Franciscan friar, De Osuna, first introduced Teresa to biblical thought and to prayer. She was favored by experiences in mystical prayer early in religious life. These were followed by many years of painful difficulties in trying to remain united to God daily. On her own admission she tried to avoid God's call to total abandonment for twenty years. Later she observed,

God arrives at times very late, but then he pays generously and with such high interest, all at once, as he has been granting to others for many years. I spent fourteen years unable to do meditation unless it were accompanied by reading (WOP, Ch. 17).

Then, in 1554, while meditating on a painting of Christ being scourged at the pillar, she was given such a liberating religious experience that she came to life once again. It was this experience and St. Augustine's **Confessions** that brought her, finally, to capitulate to God. After this her prayer became what spiritual writers called "passive quiet," that is, a state in which God actively worked in her while she remained relatively passive, simply accepting the work of God within. She also experienced the "prayer of union" in which she was conscious of her union with the Lord deep within. So extraordinary were her experiences that they were hard to describe, even to her spiritual director. As a result, this led some directors to regard them as suspect, possibly even induced by the devil. Her eventual resolution of this problem resulted in a written clarification found in the book of her **Life**.

DOCTRINE OF TERESA

To describe her journey into prayer, Teresa used the image of a castle, which is described in detail in her work, the **Interior**

Castle. In addition to this masterpiece of her **Life**, the **Way of Perfection** and the **Book of Foundations**, other small works still extant are: *Meditation on the Song of Songs, Spiritual Testimonies* (short accounts of favors and on her interior state), *Soliloquies, Dwelling Places,* her *Constitutions, Manner of Visiting Monasteries, Poetry* and some four hundred forty *Letters*. Not a trained writer as were other Spanish authors, Teresa wrote her works as she spoke to the Castilian people. The result is a spontaneous, direct, unsophisticated style sprinkled with wit and humor. She once quipped, "God deliver me from gloomy saints!" All her writings were written during the last twenty years of her life.

Basically, her doctrine is that prayer is nearness to God: "Mental prayer in my opinion is nothing else than an intimate sharing between friends; it means taking time frequently to be alone with the One we know loves us" (**Life**, Ch. 8). To do this she says those who pray must practice "recollection," so called because the "soul collects all its faculties together and enters within itself to be with its God" (**WOP**, Ch. 28). This can happen under the most mundane circumstances:

> **At one time I took advantage for my soul in seeing field, water, flowers; in those things I used to find memory of the Creator; that is, they would wake me up and recollect myself; they were as a book (Life, Ch. 9).**

Teresa also recommended vocal prayer, especially the "Our Father," carefully pointing out that it is inseparable from mental prayer because there is no such thing as prayer without full attention to Christ. Recollected vocal prayer, then, was a prelude to deeper mystical prayer.

The real richness of her thought on prayer is synthesized in the **Interior Castle**. She speaks of seven dwelling places. The first three are places lived in by the pray-er herself, who arrives there by human effort and the ordinary help of grace. The last four are occupied by those who have arrived at passive, mystical prayer. Her metaphor for prayer was based on the same imagery, describing heaven as the place of "many mansions." At the center of the castle (the seventh mansion) was the Lord lighting up all the dwelling places. Those mansions closer to the Lord were more illumined than those farther away. These descriptions were ways of describing a very complex reality: the capabilities of individuals for prayer, the different ways of prayer and the degrees of prayer. Prayer itself was the entry to the castle. Though this subject was dear to her, it was no simple task, as Teresa's first words in the Prologue indicate: "Not many things that I have been ordered to do under obedience have been as difficult for me as is this present task of writing about prayer."

Despite her lack of training in writing, Teresa's works are full of imagery which make for easy reading and understanding. In her **Life** she tells of her personal experience of prayer which is amplified in a more detailed, objective way in the **Interior Castle**: "A beginner must look on herself as one setting out to make a garden for her Lord's pleasure, on most unfruitful soil which abounds in weeds. Her Majesty roots up the weeds and will put in good plants instead..." She adds a description about the watering of this garden of prayer:

It seems to me that the garden may be watered in four different ways. Either the water must be drawn from a well, which is very laborious; or by a waterwheel and buckets, worked by a windlass...or from a stream or spring, which waters the ground much better...or by heavy rain, when the Lord waters it himself without any labor of ours; and this is an incomparably better method than all the rest (Life, Ch. 11).

Teresa knows how to bring exalted things down to our own level, down to earth!